WOMEN IN PEASANT MOVEMENTS

WOMEN IN PEASANT MOVEMENTS

Tebhaga, Naxalite and After

DEBAL K. SINGHA ROY

MANOHAR
2026

First published 1992

Reprinted 2026

ISBN 978-81-85425-73-3

Published by
Ajay Kumar Jain *for*
Manohar Publishers & Distributors
4753/23 Ansari Road, Daryaganj
New Delhi 110 002

Printed at
Replika Press Pvt. Ltd.

Dedicated to

My Parents and Prabha
inspiration behind my being and becoming

ACKNOWLEDGEMENTS

This study is partly based on my Ph.D. thesis and partly on my post doctoral study. I am grateful to a large number of persons who have extended their cooperation in completing this work. My debt in specially great to Dr. Sharit K. Bhowmik, Reader in Sociology, Delhi School of Economics, Delhi University, who offered constructive criticism and valuable guidance at every stage of preparation of this manuscript. I also thank Prof. P.N. Mukherjee, Indian Statistical Institute, New Delhi, Prof. Ramkrishna Mukherjee, Calcutta, Dr. Vina Majumdar, Centre for Women's Development Studies, New Delhi and Dr. T.K. Roy my former colleague at CWDS for their useful suggestions from time to time.

I am also extremely thankful to Prof. B.R. Chauhan the then Prof. and Head, Department of Sociology, Institute of Advanced Studies, Meerut and presently, Senior Consultant in Sociology, Indira Gandhi National Open University (IGNOU) New Delhi, without whom this work would not have been completed.

My sincere thanks are also due to Prof. Kapil Kumar, Faculty of History, Prof. S.P. Verma, Faculty of Public Administration, Prof. P.Nayak, Director, School of Social Sciences, Prof. G.S.Rao, Faculty of English Language, Dr. (Mrs.) Shobhita Jain, Faculty of Sociology, Ms. Joyoti Gupta and Ms. Alka Dhamija all from IGNOU for their stimulating suggestions and continuous support.

I presented the findings of my work at XII World Congress of Sociology in July 1990 at Madrid. Prof. V.C. Kundaiswamy the Vice-Chancellor, IGNOU gave me financial support to attend the Conference. My grateful thanks to him for his encouragement and appreciation and to Prof. Neuma Aguiar and other participants at the Congress for the interest they took in my presentation.

I owe special debt of gratitude to Mr. Santosh Rana (Ex MLA) Gopiballavpur, Mr. Sovan Pal, Somra Mardi and other Naxalite leaders of Gopiballavpur, Comprehensive Area Development Project (CADP) officials of Boinchi (Hooghli), local political leaders and social workers of Gofanagar and Khanpur (West Dinajpur) and the respondents of the villages for their generous help and hospitality during my fieldwork and to the female respondents for giving me indepth and accurate information.

I am also thankful to the staff of the National Library, Calcutta, The Nehru Memorial Museum and Library, New Delhi, Indian Statistical Institute Library, Calcutta, Jawaharlal Nehru University Library, New Delhi, Centre for Women's Development Studies Library, New Delhi and Central Secretariat Library, New Delhi for their cooperation.

I sincerely acknowledge with thanks the Doctoral Fellowship awarded to me by the Indian Council for Social Science Research (ICSSR) to undertake this study.

My brother Benoy K. Singha Roy always took keen interest in my work. I am highly thankful to him. I owe a special debt to my wife Prabha for her sustained support during the preparation of the manuscript.

IGNOU
New Delhi

DEBAL K. SINGHA ROY

CONTENTS

I

INTRODUCTION

The Problem

In a predominantly agricultural society women's role in the production process is crucial, their household and reproductive activities providing the basis for the productive activities. Both in terms of subsistence activity and reproduction of children that provide hands to maintain the system they perform important economic role (Eircksen and Klein 1981: 293). They earn for the family and contribute to the production and marketing of products of agriculture and handicraft (CSWI 1974:4). This is apart from their contribution to housekeeping by doing the household chores. In transitional agrarian societies, women's roles become even more complex and diversified. The dynamism that the trends of land reform, agricultural modernisation, peasant movement, political mobilisation and so on bring about is reflected in the women's socio-economic roles.

The normative structure of agrarian society, however, ascribes an unequal position to women. These women, who are mostly illiterate and belong to the lower castes or tribes, are economically marginalised with negligible or nil access to productive resources, are subject to wage discrimination, are socially subjugated and are politically powerless group, unrepresented or under-represented in decision-making bodies. Their contribution to the household economy and to society is often undervalued and goes unrecognised. The societal norms and values of patriarchy, caste and ethnicity and values of female subordination and sex segregation, perpetuate the inferior position of the female.

It was inevitable that the enforced submission of such women would lead to accumulation of latent discontent among them. And when the opportunity arose for them to realise that they were a force to reckon with, their pent-up discontent manifested itself in militant forms. Women participated in a big way in peasant movements and mass mobilisation for collective action. The manifestations of their discontent were not uniform, their response to such movements being widely shaped by the latter's ideology and the broad process of socio-political formation of the agrarian society that fostered them.

This study endeavours to understand the role working class rural women played in peasant movements at different levels of the economic and political formation of an agrarian society. With its focus on West Bengal, it specifically seeks to examine:

(a) the form and extent of working-class rural women's response to the extensive peasant movements (namely the Tebhaga Movement of 1946-47 and the Naxalite Movement of 1967-71) and to the process of collective mobilisation in contemporary peasant movement (of the 1970s and 1980s);
(b) the changes in their response to the process of collective mobilisation of the peasantry; and
(c) the major factors affecting their responses to peasant movements.

The Agrarian Dynamics of West Bengal: An Overview

On the eve of the Tebhaga Movement of 1946-47 the agrarian society of Bengal was highly stratified and disintegrated, the seeds of this stratification having been sown as early as 1793 when the British introduced the Permanent Settlement Act. The new legislation replaced most of the old Zamindars by new ones drawn largely from urban traders, money-lenders, etc. who had acquired wealth and influence doing business with the Company. The new system, which was basically calculated to give the colonial government scope for the extraction of a part of the surplus in the form of land revenue (Chatterjee 1982 : 148), deprived the actual cultivators of their traditional rights including the right of security of tenure (NCA 1976:3), gave the Zamindars unabated scope to exploit the peasantry (Chaudhuri 1977:16), and made agriculture more market-oriented (Islam 1978:1). The self-sufficient peasantry gave way to a disintegrating village community system of production, paving the way for exploitative employer-employee relations in the agrarian society (Mukherjee 1933: 527).

Assessing the impact of British rule in India Marx wrote: "The historical pages of their rule in India report hardly anything beyond destruction" (Marx 1976: 495). This is supported by the report of the Land Revenue Commission in 1940 :

> When the Britishers came and assumed administration of Bengal, she had cotton, silk and salt industries on a large scale. Company's trading policy depressed those industries. Since permanent settlement, it was Bengal's surplus which met the expense of wars for the consolidation of British rule in India (LRC Vol. 1:261).

Within the framework of this destroyed economy, the agrarian social scene also disintegrated, giving rise to a series of intermediaries under different names between the tiller of the soil and government. Some of these intermediaries were Zamindars, Talukdars, Naibs, Patnidars, Izaradars, Dar-patnidars, Dar-Izaradars, Se-patnidars, Se-Izaradars, and Bhadralok Jotedars (absentee landlords). A class of cultivators also grew who were either Ryoti-Jotedars or rich farmers, while the class of agricultural workers disintegrated into sharecroppers and agricultural labourers. A non-agricultural class also arose comprising money-lenders and traders.

Landholding having become extremely subinfeudated, the lowest strata of agrarian hierarchy were reduced to dire straits, while the class of intermediaries, cultivators and the non-agricultural class accumulated substantial income and profit from the agrarian economy. The deteriorating economic condition of the lowest strata was reflected in the rapid expansion in the number of sharecroppers and agricultural labourers in the Bengal agrarian society of the time.

The spread of sharecroppers (Bargadars or Bhagchasis) was interlinked with the indebtedness of small owner cultivators to the village money-lenders, traders and other intermediaries. Traders, money-lenders and intermediary landowners exploited up to the hilt the poverty of the poor peasant and lent him money at usurious rates of interest. When the poor peasant, unable to repay the debt lost his land to the creditor, he was resettled on the same land on condition that he paid half of the produce to the creditor. The Report of the Land Revenue Commission in 1940 observed that of 8,547,004 enquired acres all over the province, 592,335 acres were transferred, of which 31.7 per cent was turned over to *Barga* and

24.6 per cent to under-tenants (LRC 1940, Vol. 2: 120).

Peasants who mortgaged their land but were not settled on it as sharecroppers became agricultural labourers. The growing impoverishment in rural Bengal can be estimated from the fact that whereas in 1901 agricultural labourers formed only 17.5 per cent of the rural population between 1920 and 1931 their proportion increased by 49 per cent (Sen 1979:35). The Land Revenue Commission pointed out in 1940 that agricultural labourers constituted 22.5 per cent of the total number of families of Bengal (LRC 1940, Vol. 2: 117-120): Clearly, poverty was becoming more extensive. The Famine Commission in 1945 reported that there were 7.5 million families holding less than two acres of land. About two million families (about 10 million people) were dependent on agricultural wages, Bargadars comprising one million people (RFC 1945: 5). The Commission also pointed out the miserable plight of families holding less than five acres of land.

Rural society is conveniently classified into three classes, class I comprising landholders and supervisory farmers, class II being composed of self-sufficient peasantry, artisans and traders, and class III consisting of sharecroppers and agricultural labourers. During the period under discussion, in the rural society of Bengal the proportion of class I and class III increased at the expense of class II (Mukherjee 1957: 227), the landlord-tenant-sharecropper sector having become most dominant (Dhanagare 1976: 362). To begin with, this relationship was favoured by the impoverished for two reasons: (a) it secured them employment throughout the year, and (b) as sharecroppers the peasants still remained 'grihasthas' or husbandmen and therefore socially they ranked on par with the ryot (Mukherjee 1957: 49-50). The exploitation and social oppression of the peasantry became institutionalised in course of time, with rack-renting, subinfeudation, fragmentation of holdings, indebtedness, increasing taxation, increasingly unfavourable market manipulation, decreasing real wage of agricultural labourers, and the gradual impoverishment and pauperisation of the peasantry becoming prominent characteristics of the society of the time (Rasul 1974: 1).

While the newly formed political parties of peasant origin, namely the Peasants and Workers Party and Krishak Praja Party took note of the peasants' deteriorating condition in the 1920s, no systematic plan of action was undertaken either for the uplift of the poor peasantry or for their collective mobilisation until 1936, when the Bengal Kisan Sabha, the provincial unit of the All India Kisan Sabha, was formed. The launch of this party was, indeed, a landmark in the history of peasant movement in

Bengal. Its manifesto proclaimed its objective to be to secure complete freedom from exploitation and achieve full economic and political power for the peasants and workers. The Kisan Sabha began to radicalise its agrarian programme from the early 1940s and it began to mobilise the sharecroppers for attaining '*Tebhaga*' (two-thirds of the share to the sharecroppers), a demand that already had been accepted in 1940 by the Land Revenue Commission. The Sabha passed a resolution in Calcutta, in November 1946, for Tebhaga struggle and for the mobilisation of sharecroppers (Sen 1979: 118).

The mounting discontent of the lower strata of the peasantry and the emerging political processes of the late colonial period culminated in the peasant movements of Bengal on the eve of Independence, most prominent of which was the Tebhaga Movement of 1946-47.

Agrarian Society of West Bengal: 1947-67

In the truncated Bengal that remained as India's share after independence, the Congress Party government that came to power under the Chief Ministership of Dr. Bidhan Chandra Roy initiated a radical land reform legislation. The West Bengal Estate Acquisition Act (1953) was intended to abolish the Zamindari and other intermediary systems and the West Bengal Land Reform Act (1955) to put a ceiling on landholding, to allow 60 per cent of the produced share to the sharecroppers and to put restriction on the eviction of sharecroppers except for self-cultivation by the landowners. Often, however, these far-reaching proposals merely remained in the statute books. Initially, the tenants were either unaware of the new legislation or were too weak both economically and socially to insist on their rights (Report of the Panel on the Land Reform Committee 1956: 40). There was widespread malafide land transfer resulting in the eviction of sharecroppers, their lapse into the category of agricultural labourers, and loss of tenurial and employment security to the agrarian downtrodden. It was also obvious that the political will to implement the egalitarian legislation was lacking (Ghosh and Dutta 1977: 164, Bardhan and Rudra 1980: 1945, Dasgupta 1984: 86).

According to the report of the National Sample Survey of 1954-55, which was unaffected by the ceiling restriction, 20.5 per cent of the households were landless; 65.5 per cent of the households had less than five acres of land and occupied only 34.5 per cent of the total land; whereas 5.4 per cent households occupied as much as 40 per cent of the total land. Sharecroppers constituted 16 per cent of the rural households. In 1961-62, the proportion of landless households dropped significantly to 12.6 per cent, while sharecropper households came down to 2.9 per cent. Households owning more than 10 acres of land came down to 4.1 per cent and the area they owned also came down to 27.7 per cent. Again, in 1971-72, the proportion of landless and sharecropper households came down to 10.8 and 2 per cent respectively, while the percentage of households owning more than 10 acres of land was reduced to 2.5 and they occupied only 18.9 per cent of the total land. The proportion of households owning less than 2.50 acres of land and owning between 2.50 to 9.99 acres changed from 52.9 and 21.2 per cent, respectively, in 1954-55 to 66.8 and 19.9 per cent respectively in 1971-72. Significantly enough, in the period under review their area of landholding also had increased from 15.8 to 27.7 per cent and from 44.2 to 53.4 per cent, respectively.

Table 1.1: Landholding and Sharecropping in West Bengal
(A comparative picture of 1954-55, 1961-62 and 1971-72)

Category (in acres)	Percentage of Rural Households			Percentage of Area Owned (in acres)		
	1954-55	1961-62	1971-72	1954-55	1961-62	1971-72
Landless Households	20.5	12.6	10.8	—	—	—
Share-croppers	16.0	2.9	2.0	—	—	—
Households owning below 2.50	52.9	56.7	66.8	15.8	17.5	27.7
Households owning between 2.50 and 9.99	21.2	26.6	19.9	44.2	54.8	53.4
Households owning above 10.00	5.4	4.1	2.5	40.0	27.7	18.9

Source: NSS, 1954-55, 1961-62, 1971-72.

The period between 1947 and 1967 was marked by deteriorating socio-economic status of the lowest section of the agrarian hierarchy of West Bengal, though apparently the extent of landlessness had decreased and the proportion of small and medium cultivators had increased. The upper strata still managed to hold on to their socio-economic privileges. The difficulty posed by the abolition of the intermediary system was skirted by the big landowners (the old intermediaries and their allies) by resorting to malafide land transfer in the names of family members and relatives. In the absence of adequate legal protection sharecroppers still had to put up with eviction, low share in the crops they had raised, low wages (in the case of agricultural labourers), and increasing indebtedness. Pressure on land had meanwhile increased enormously due to sluggish industrial development, bleak alternative sources of employment for the rural people, and increasing immigration from East Pakistan (now Bangladesh). Census data show that in 1961, of the total main workers 38.5 per cent were cultivators and 15.30 per cent were agricultural labourers, while in 1971, the percentage of cultivators came down to 32 per cent and that of agricultural labourers rose sharply to 26 per cent (Census of India, 1961, 1971). Obviously a rapid shift was taking place, indicating a heightening of disparities in the rural society.

In 1967 the Leftist-dominated United Front Government came to power. It was also the year when for the first time after independence West Bengal experienced a vehement manifestation of peasant discontent in the form of the Naxalite Movement. The Naxalite Movement began with the Marxist-Leninist-Maoist ideological framework that advocated mass struggle and seizure of power by guerrilla warfare (Mukherjee 1978). As a form of radical peasant mobilisation and extreme collective action, the movement hit the national and international headlines. With this movement West Bengal's agrarian society entered into a new era of peasant struggle.

Contemporary Agrarian Society of West Bengal

The Naxalite uprising called for a rethinking on land reform laws, and the political commitment to implement these laws and rural development strategies. The Congress Ministry enacted a few radical land reform laws in 1972. The Left Front government, which later came to power activated the programme for the rapid implementation of land reform laws. Mass mobilisation was also initiated among the rural people. The result has been to bring about a change in the pre-existing agrarian processes. Since the early 1970s the sharp downward mobility of the lowest section of the agrarian society of West Bengal has been reduced. The percentage of rural labour households with land has increased from 31.2 in 1964-65 to 36.5 in 1974-75 (Rural Labour Enquiry, 1975). The 1981 Census also shows considerable increase in the percentage of cultivators and a marginal decrease in the category of landless agricultural labourers.

Rural Women and Transition of Agrarian Society

All phases of transition of an agrarian society have direct bearing on the form and extent of female work participation in agricultural activities and on their social relations of production in agriculture. A large portion of the female work force of West Bengal has remained in agriculture to support themselves. In 1931 around 47 per cent of the total female work force of West Bengal was in the agricultural sector, and their work participation rate in this sector increased to 52.4 per cent in 1951 and further to 58 per cent in 1961. The percentage, however, started falling in the 1970s and 80s (56.6 per cent in 1971 and 53.1 per cent in 1981) (Census figures).

The increase in the earlier decades was on account of increasing poverty and the decrease in the later decades was on account of their marginal shift from agricultural to non-agricultural activities, gradual involvement in intra-mural activities, and displacement of the female work force from agriculture in some agriculturally developed regions of West Bengal. Census bias also has excluded a large portion of the female work force in agriculture from the category of "worker".

Female agricultural workers have been an important constituent of the agrarian social structure of West Bengal. They have played a crucial role in all phases of the society's transition, including the agricultural modernisation and economic development of the rural society and in peasant movements and political mobilisation of the peasantry. Their mobilisation for collective action at different stages of society's transition has, however, been diverse. In periods of extensive peasant movements they were radically mobilised to bring about change in the agrarian social structure through non-institutionalised means, whereas contemporary mobilisation is done through the institutionalised framework of political parties.

The Study Design

Four villages were selected from North and South Bengal, two from each region. One each of these villages had been witness to organised peasant movement, the other being a contemporary village with similar characteristics. The celebrated Khanpur village of West Dinajpur district, where the Tebhaga Movement took place in 1947, was selected from North Bengal, and from South Bengal village Shalgeriya of Midnapur district which witnessed the extreme form of Naxalite Movement in 1969-71. Since Shalgeriya has remained agriculturally backward, Gofanagar, a village in West Dinajpur in North Bengal with similar socio-economic features was selected in the second category. Both villages lack assured irrigation facilities, have small scale or nil HYV and multicrop cultivation, have a predominance of traditional and monocrop cultivation, have adopted scientific tools and technology only to a small extent and have a substantial proportion of Scheduled Castes and Tribal population.

Similarly, since Khanpur of North Bengal is an agriculturally developed village, the agriculturally developed village Panpara from the Hooghly district in South Bengal was selected. Both villages have assured irrigation facilities, high rate of HYV, multicrop and cash crop cultivation, high extent of scientific tools and technology adoption, elaborate institutional network to help the villagers for agricultural development and have multi-caste or ethnic compositions. The selection was made after an intensive tour of these areas and in consultation with government officials, political party workers and academics.

Data collection was done in three stages and completed in ten months including pre-testing. The field study was done in the months of February to June and October to December, 1985 and June, July, 1986.

Establishing rapport with rural women, who are conservative in outlook and sensitive and respectful of outsiders is a difficult task, much more so for a male. The author had to overcome their hesitation and their husbands' resistance.

Resistance also came from certain political party workers to collect data on the political affairs of the village. There were also problems of the villagers misconstruing the author's intentions and official obstruction to data collection from the field besides food and shelter problems. By spending some time amidst the surroundings it was possible to overcome some of the resistance and secretiveness.

Interviews were conducted mostly at night. Day time was unsuitable being the time of work and others' presence which influenced the respondents' statements. Though many a time at night the male members or the presence of drunken males hampered the interviews, no other suitable time could be thought of for an effective and indepth fact-finding interview. Schedule, unstructured interview, non-participant observation and case study were the major techniques used to collect information from the selected universe.

A *schedule* was prepared for intensive household survey and finalised after pre-testing and consultations with experts. It was designed to collect detailed household information relating to total population by age, sex, education, occupation, indebtedness, landholdings (present and past), sale and purchase of land and other assets, types of crop cultivation, types of labour requirement, terms of work contract for male and female, working days of each member by sex, mode of wage payment, nature of alternative economic activities available for the female, agricultural implements and livestock and caste and ethnic background. The schedule was applied for intensive household survey of these villages.

Unstructured interview was used especially to interview working class women to cover at least 50 per cent of the female workers. Prominent labour leaders and party workers in the same or nearby villages and female participants of peasant movements were also interviewed by this method, the latter in great detail. The technique was used also to get an insight into employer-employee relations, nature and extent of female participation in the peasant unrest and political mobilisation.

The types of daily activities of the working class women were observed by non-participant observation. Their participation in agricultural labour strike, in party meetings and processions, their working hours in the field, the technology of production, the overt cultural activities of different groups and intercaste, intra-caste, intergroup and intra-group interactions were also observed.

Information regarding some important and relevant happenings in these villages was collected through *case study* technique. Besides the case studies of the two important peasant uprisings in the two villages, agricultural workers' strike, employer-employee conflict, eviction of sharecroppers, loss of lands due to indebtedness have also been studied by this method.

Clarification of the Term Workers

In the category of workers (working force) all those persons have been included who are occupied and whose occupation appeared to be related to the productive activities. Here besides those who are commonly related to productive activities (viz. cultivation, agricultural wage earnings, construction work, business, shop-keeping, cycle makers, pottery, smithery etc.) who are aslso related to regular fodder and forest produce collection have been included in the category of workers. Willingness, physical capacity and social recognition to work were the major criteria in defining a worker.

II

THEORETICAL FRAMEWORK

The position of women in the family and society in general and in the production process in particular has been an important concern of social scientists. R.H. Lowie (1920: 48) was probably the first to bring a systematic discussion on the status of women in society into social anthropological literature. Basing himself on his study of primitive societies he made a few significant generalisations. He observed that where women do most of the agricultural work they receive bride-wealth but where their work participation is limited or negligible the girl's family has to pay the boy's family.

A.R. Radcliffe-Brown (1922: 74) observed that in the Andaman island the women's status is equal to that of men. B. Malinowzki (1927: 11) also found in the Trobriands that the position of woman is not servile to her husband; she has her own possessions and public and private sphere of influence. G.P. Murdock (1949: 205) described the position of women on a higher cultural level where women get approximately equal status in society under sedentary conditions of life. He also observed that the introduction of agriculture lifts women's economic contribution to a level above that of the men. W.J. Goode (1968: 202) stated that in Tikopia male authority is neither significantly powerful nor sacred: the wife may scold the husband and may even resort to physical violence at times.

Classical social anthropologists and sociologists viewed women's position in terms of broad theoretical perspectives. Levi-Strauss (1949: 469) for example, perceived women as a 'sign' and pointed out that they should be exchanged like 'things' to overcome the contradiction between two incompatible aspects: personal desire and desire of others and was seen as the means of binding others through alliance with them.

The Marxist view on women's issues has been a subject of controversy. The earlier Marxists believed that women's economic oppression resulted from their 'disadvantaged position in the labour market' following from their household responsibility. But with the recognition that "labour went on within the family" and "by extending the scope of economics to include most women's labour it was hoped to provide a materialist account of women's oppression" (Bottomore et al. 1983: 135). Engels (1976: 226-39) blamed private property as the root cause of the initial oppression of women in human society. To him, increase of wealth created entirely new social relationships depriving women of their traditional rights. The communistic household recognised the supremacy of the mother in the house, "just as the exclusive recognition of a natural mother" and high esteem for women in society. In the communistic household, he writes:

> "Women occupied not only a free but also a highly respected position among all savages and all barbarians of the lower and middle stages and partly even of the upper stage" (1976: 226).

Nevertheless, as a result of the development of economic conditions of life, introduction of pairing families (one man and one woman) through monogamous marriage, and possession of private wealth by the pairing families, the status of women and especially the concept of mother-right was severely affected. To quote Engels:

> Pairing marriage had introduced a new element into the family. By the side of the natural mother it had placed the authenticated natural father.... According to the division of labour... the procuring of food and the implements necessary thereto, and therefore, also, the ownership of the latter, fell to the man; he took them with him in case of separation, just as the woman retained the household goods. Thus... the man was also the owner of new sources of foodstuff... the cattle—and later of the new instrument of labour—the slaves (1976: 231).

According to 'mother-right', however, children could not inherit from their father. The children belonged to their mother's gens, and inherited from the mother. When the owner of the herd died, his properties were inherited by his brothers and sisters and their children or by the descendants of his mother's sisters. Hence Engels writes:

> as wealth increased, it, on the one hand, gave the man a more important status in the family than the women, and, on the other hand created a stimulus to utilise the strengthened position in order to overthrow the traditional order of inheritance in favour of his children. But it was not possible as long as descent according to mother right prevailed. It had therefore to be overthrown and it was overthrown.... The overthrow of mother right was the world historic defeat of the female sex. The man seized the reins in the home also, the woman was degraded, enthralled, the slave of man's lust, a mere instrument, for breeding children (1976: 232-33).

Emile Durkheim (1933: 56-60) offers a sociological analysis of the sexual division of labour and perceives it as a source of "conjugal solidarity", whereby one sex takes care of the "effective" and the other the "intellectual functions". The most remarkable effect, he perceives, is that "it renders them solidarity".

Max Weber (1958: 62) develops a correlation between the development of capitalism and the presence of the spirit of rational self-control among some sections of women. He locates women workers with the capitalist spirit only among girls having a "pietistic background". They have the best chances of economic education, feeling of obligation to their job and a cool self-control which are necessary 'for the conception of labour as an end in itself as a calling'.

On the whole, the early social anthropologists and sociologists, while they have provided important perspectives for broad generalisations have not given adequate attention to the question of women's status and work participation in society. Studies with specific focus on women started with Alva Myrdal's noted work, *Nation and the Family*. This study stressed women's economic role in the national life, and the socio-economic constraints therein. She mentioned that the "remuneration (of women) is only slightly related to efficiency of work and is largely determined by the goodwill and capacity of the husband" (Myrdal 1941: 398). In another work Alva Myrdal and Klein (1968: 2) described the role of women as "home maker" and "producer". They recognised the large-scale entry of women in the labour market as the "recovering of women's lost territory". E. Boulding (1967) in her work presented a "macro-history" on the socio-economic perspectives of women. She identified the "victim position of women" in historical records as having resulted from the "under-estimation of the role of household in society".

In her celebrated study, *Women's Role in Economic Development*,

E. Boserup (1970) described the persisting sexual division of labour and the fundamental role of women in African agriculture and their lesser roles in Asian agriculture and Latin America as well. She also provided the basis for an explanation based on the African system of shifting and Asian system of plough cultivation. She pointed out that introduction of modern technology in the regions under plough cultivation has discouraged the female's involvement in agricultural operation and "encouraged segregation of the sexes, including the seclusion of women in some areas". In her study on Africa, W. Maloba (1983: 316) found two levels of exploitation of the peasant women there, namely, belonging to an oppressed class and being women. She described the peasant woman of Africa as a "toiling being" where the frustrated husband, the helpless hungry children, all cry on her shoulder, making her suffer equally for every misfortune that every member of the family faces. The study by K.M. Woodsmall (1960) highlighted the socio-economic lives of rural women in Asia and their double burden of house and daily toil in the field.

Women Studies in India

In India, the need for women studies was felt only after the U.N. General Assembly made the Declaration of the Elimination of Discrimination Against Women in 1967, and subsequently requested U.N. member states to submit a report on the status of women in their countries. The setting up of the Committee on the Status of Women in India (CSWI) in 1971 in pursuance of this request has become a landmark for women studies in India. In response to the "U.N. Call for Action" in 1975 and on the basis of the findings of the Committee on the Status of Women (1974) the Government of India then drew up a Draft National Plan of Action for Women. The plan accords priority to the need of purposive research in education, health, welfare and employment of women, with special emphasis on the weaker section of women whose conditions were most adversely affected by the process of social change and unbalanced economic development. The Indian Council of Social Science Research (ICSSR) also has recognised the status of women as a priority area for research and has commissioned a programme on women's studies with emphasis on the poorer or the less visible sections of society (ICSSR 1977: 7-10). The University Grants Commission (UGS) also has set up Women Studies Development Centres in various universities.

Bina Agarwal (1983: 8) in a review study points out that in recent years, the focus of research on women has shifted substantially from preoccupation with women's role in the family marriage and kinships network to their participation in the economic sphere.

Women in Agriculture: An Overview of their Status

The initial focus on women in the labour force was reflected in D.R. Gadgil's (1924) well-known study *Industrial Evolution of India in Recent Times*. The varied rates of women's participation in economic activity and associated factors like caste, ethnic background, economic pressure etc. were also brought together by him in another study. Gadgil (1965: 27) noted that the pace of economic development did not yet appear to influence women's employment significantly in India. R.S. Woodsmall (1960: 295) located women's position in the production process and asserted that in the Indian countryside women are an "economic asset". The Committee on the Status of Women (1974: 49) highlighted several important socio-economic features of work participation of women. The report points out that among the marginal and landless agriculturists earning a livelihood is still a family endeavour with or without division of labour between men and women.

L. Gulati (1978: 32), presenting the socio-economic profile of female agricultural labourers, points out the phenomenon of concentration of women workers in agriculture in spite of low wages and wage discrimination. The life history of a female agricultural labourer called Kalyani suggests that "Kalyani's mother and father were both agricultural labourers, so is Kalyani ... Kalyani's two daughters join the labour market like their mother". The study by V. Mazumdar, K. Sharma and S. Acharya (1979: 11) reveals the relationship between land, labour and capital and the location of the rural women's lives in the rural social structure. The study depicts the situation of poverty, lower social status, illiteracy and ill health of these women, for whom wage discrimination is more a rule than an exception. G. Kelkar and S. Anandalakshmy (1980: 65) find in a village of Rajasthan that in spite of the substantial contribution of women in the rural economy they have been subject to marginality and subordinate status, their productive role having been viewed as secondary to their reproductive role. The relationships between rural women's work participation, the extent of their poverty and economic invisibility have been brought out in a study by Parthasarathy and Rao (1981: 136). The study suggests that a high participation rate of women in the labour force reflects the poorer economic and lower social status of their household; a low participation rate, on the other hand, reflects a higher economic invisibility of their work. R.M. Sethi (1982: 134) reveals that female work participation in agriculture is not favoured by the traditional values of the Punjabis but economic compulsion pushes them into the labour market.

Most studies reveal the unfavourable, discriminating and exploitative working conditions of rural women. K.M. Manohar aptly summarises:

> Studies conducted in several parts of India indicate the awful conditions of the women workers in this sector (agricultural). It is found that a significant percentage of these jobs are manned by women drawn from lower caste and lower class.... Ignorance, tradition bound attitudes, illiteracy, lack of skills, seasonal nature of employment, heavy physical work of different types, discrimination in the wage structure ... lack of guarantee of minimum wages, lack of job security, lack of comprehensive legislation to cover these workers in unorganised sector ... ill treatment, migration and disintegration of families, bondage and alienation etc. are some of the characteristics of employment in this sector. Although these jobs offer no attraction and require a great deal of physical ordeal, large number of women continue to search for these jobs for their livelihood over the years only to taste disrespect, slavery and ill health (Manohar 1982: 8-18).

Kalpana Bardhan (1985: 2207) highlights the structural elements of society that are responsible for economic exploitation, which in turn makes the women labourers subject to sexual exploitation and to socially cordoned, culturally rationalised discrimination and exclusion even within their class. Developmental activities, land reform and modern technology have also brought severe adverse impact on rural women. K. Saradamoni (1983: 91) shows that land reforms and cash crop brought substantial change in the rural social structure in Palghat district of Kerala. But women have been the greatest losers in the land reform process, many of them having lost access over the productive resources, and also the traditional avenues of their employment. The study by B. Agarwal (1984: 48) suggests that HYV (high yielding variety) rice cultivation has not benefited rural women. P. Law's findings also bear this out. In his study on the impact of the green revolution on women he points out (1985: 84) that agricultural modernisation has increased class and sex polarisation adversely affecting rural women.

The persisting awful working conditions, increasing economic insecurity and deteriorating socio-economic status have caused enormous discontent among the women workers in agriculture. This discontent has manifested in the form of their spontaneous participation in the organized peasant movements. However, one significant area of women studies which has remained relatively less explored is women's participation in the peasant movement and political mobilisation. The heroic roles they played in all phases of the development of a movement remained under or unrecorded and unrecognised in social science literature. Though a few important studies have emerged, this area still requires more investigation.

Gail Omvedt (1977: 370-398) made an important analysis of the role of rural women in the rural revolt in India. The interconnections between the class and sexual oppression and between women's movement and class struggle have been analysed in this study in terms of the key concepts of work participation and mode of production. She points out:

> The change in agricultural class relations, and the growing self-assertiveness of agricultural labourers and poor peasants resulting from it have led to the growing militancy of working women in India and to a growing consciousness of women's oppression and the importance of the fight against it. Today it is possible to say that a women's movement has begun in, at least, some crucial areas of India.

P. Custers (1986: 97-103) who has studied the role of women in the Tebhaga Movement of Bengal examines the important questions pertaining to the unbroken male dominance over leadership. The study points out that the poor rural women participated not only in harvesting paddy, encircling cutcheries of Jotedars, and in facing police repression, they also gave precious leadership to the uprising in its roughest phase. "It was primarily through her militancy and concrete struggle experience that women raised the need for female volunteers, for *nari bahini*. On the whole, this creation happened spontaneously". Regarding women's leadership this study points out that:

> Patriarchal ideas are entrenched in the tradition and theories of liberation movements themselves. Because people in general do not change their ideas easily, and because it goes against male interests to be frank, the overhauling of revolutionary ideology undoubtedly will not happen without a very tough struggle.

In her study R. Chakravarty (1980) mentioned the extent of participation of women in the communist movement in India in general and in the communist-led peasant movements in particular. A. Basu (1981: 218) has studied the nature and form of women's participation in the political protest of West Bengal and Maharashtra. The study highlights that in contemporary West Bengal institutionalised women's participation in peasant movements has replaced the early form of militancy. T. Sarkar (1984: 96) in her study points out the condition and meaning of women's participation in political protest. She finds that there seems to be a definite equivalence between the potential for politicisation and a direct involvement in the production process. Sunil Sen (1984: 195) studies the involvement of working women in popular movements and women's organisations in West Bengal. He makes a brief historical survey of peasant struggle of Bengal and highlights the nature and extent of women's participation in the Independence Movement, Tebhaga Movement, Naxalite Movement and their involvement in various women's organisations.

Studies show that patterns of women's responses to crisis in society differ from each other. Their participation in politics increases sharply in crises and declines during normal times (C.W.D.S. 1987: 21).

A broad conceptual understanding based on indepth empirical investigation on the changing role and status of women in the broad processes of agrarian transformation and class formation is yet to take place in India. Also, similar understanding is yet to emerge on the changing form and extent of women's participation in the peasant movement and political mobilisation in agrarian society. The socio-economic roles played by women in rural society and the facets of their responses to collective mobilisation have been diversified. The important diversifications have been delineated based on the levels of agricultural modernisation, occupational diversification and economic development.

With the growing thrust for knowledge on rural and agrarian dynamics a significant body of literature of agrarian studies has emerged in recent years. Using sophisticated theoretical perspectives and indepth empiricism these studies have focused on the impact of rural technological changes, Green Revolution, rural-urban continuum and changing patterns of stratification systems. An important facet of these studies has been agrarian class analysis using a wide range of conceptual perspectives and theoretical approaches.

Daniel Thorner (1956) has identified proprietors (Maliks), working peasants (Kishans) and labourers (Majdoors) to be the prominent agrarian classes in India. To B. Kotovsky (1964) these classes are the bourgeoisie landowners, sharecroppers and agricultural labourers. Andre Beteille

(1974) classified them in terms of landlords, owner-cultivators, tenants, sharecroppers and agricultural labourers. J. Mencher (1974) identified these classes as the landless poor peasants, middle peasants, rich farmers, capitalist farmers, traditional landlords and intermediary class of large landholders. To H. Alavi (1975) bourgeoisie landowners, colonial landowners, sharecroppers and agricultural labourers are the major agrarian classes in India. N. Chandra (1975) identifies them to be the upper class landed families including landlords, Jotedars, rich peasants, marginal peasants; and lower class families including poor peasants and agricultural labourers. To J. Harris (1977) capitalist farmers, rich peasants, independent middle peasants and poor peasants are the major agrarian classes. According to Ashok Rudra (1978) the class of big landowners and the class of agricultural labourers have emerged as the major agrarian categories or classes in India in the process of agrarian transformation.

Agrarian transformation is another important facet of agrarian studies in India, and in the last two decades major debates on the modes of production in agriculture have dominated the field. Two broad lines of transformation have been elucidated, namely the "development of capitalist relations" and the "persistence of semi-feudal or feudal mode of production in agriculture". G. Kotovsky (1964), D. Thorner (1969 and 1980), A. Rudra (1971 and 1974), U. Patnaik (1971 and 1974), P. Chattopadhyay (1972), J. Banaji (1972), Ghosh and Dutta (1972), and A. Thorner (1982) have pointed out the "capitalistic" form of agrarian transformation in India. Their main points of argument for capitalist development have been large-scale farming, modernisation, mechanisation and commoditisation of agriculture, surplus capital accumulation and its reinvestment for profits and minimisation of the importance of extra-economic nexus in agriculture. On the other hand, A. Bhaduri (1973), P. Prasad (1973), N. Chandra (1974) have emphasised the persistence of "semi-feudal" legacy in agriculture in the eastern parts of the country. The crux of their arguments is based on the wide-scale use of traditional and backward technology, predominance of sharecropping system of cultivation, extra-economic coercion, and the reactionary role of usurers' capital in agriculture. Some noted scholars have emphasised the unique form of agrarian transformation in India. H. Alavi (1975) has noticed the predominance of colonial mode of production in India, while Andre Beteille (1974) has pointed out the emergence of "progressive farmers" in the northern part of the country. H. Hayami (1981) has observed the emergence of the 'middle and upper strata of the peasantry" in various parts of India.

The whole gamut of agrarian transformation has also affected the process of class transformation in the agrarian society of India. Following the Marxian frame of class analysis, T.J. Byres (1981) has conceptualised the process of class formation as the transformation of "class-in-itself" to "class-for-itself" and P.N. Mukherjee (1981) has perceived this as the transformation of 'social categories" into "social classes".

These studies, while they have made significant contibutions towards an understanding of rural stratification and the dynamics of agrarian reality, have not looked into the position of women in agriculture as a distinctive and separate entity in the processes of class formation and agrarian transformation. Women form a separate analytical and empirical category and at the same time are distinct from the more commonly used categories of class, race, caste and so on. Frequently, women are an especially oppressed group within each unit of socio-economic stratification (Agarwal 1989: 1). The process of agrarian social transformation has affected the economic and political role and status of rural working women in a distinctively separate way. Women have distinct social and economic positions. Hence, they are required to be treated separately for an indepth understanding of the dynamics of rural social formation in general and of the role and status of women in the processes of social transformations in particular. This separate identity is of vital importance in the context of a study on the form and direction of women's response to the peasant movements at different phases of the transition of society.

Peasant Movements: Search for a Perspective

The study of peasant movements has been an emerging area of social science enquiry in recent years. Social scientists from various disciplines like sociology, social anthropology, history, economics, political science and also the activists and leaders of various movements have shown an increasing interest in the study of peasant movements. The scholars have viewed peasant movements as a distinct variant of social movement and have endeavoured to analyse these in terms of their linkages with social change and class conflict, while applying the broad analytical perspectives used in the study of social movements to conceptualise, analyse and to identify the genesis of peasant movements. (Rao 1979, Dhanagare 1986).

Social movement has been broadly perceived as an organised or collective effort *to bring about changes* in the thought, beliefs, values, attitudes, relationships and major institutions in society or to *resist any change* in any of the above structural elements of society. H. Blumer

(1946) defines social movement as "collective enterprises to establish a new social order of life". C.W. King (1956) defines it as a "group venture which aims to inaugurate changes in thought, behaviour and social relationship". To H. Toch (1965) a social movement is an "effort by a large number of people to solve collectively a problem they feel they have in common". According to R. Haberle (1972) it is "a collective attempt to bring about a change in certain social institutions or to create an entirely new order." J.R. Gusfield (1972) perceives a social movement as a socially shared demand for change in some aspects of the social order. To J. Wilson (1973) a social movement is an "organised attempt to bring about or resist large-scale changes in the social order by non-institutionalised means".

Most of these definitions view social movements as organised and intended collective actions. These actions are based on certain defined aims, methodology for collective mobilisation, distinctive ideology and identified leadership and organisation. Social scientists are in agreement that three elements are basic to a social movement. These are: collective mobilisation; an ideology and an orientation towards change. (Rao 1983: 12).

Following from the above we may define a peasant movement as an organised and collective attempt of the peasantry (subsistence and small producers, sharecroppers and agricultural labourers) to bring about change in the pattern of ownership, control and use of land, share of agricultural produce, wage structure, credit and institutional support system and in other aspects of socio-economic life that have subjugated them over a period of time. The aspects of the form and direction of collective mobilisation, ideology and orientation towards change of a peasant movement are closely interrelated and interdependent. The combination of these three elements plays a crucial role in the dynamics of a peasant movement. Change in the form of these elements, however, brings tremendous change in the character of a peasant movement. The form and extent of response of the rural masses towards a peasant movement largely depend on the character of these basic elements of the movement.

A movement is identified by the form of collective mobilisation and its direction towards change. P.N. Mukherjee (1979: 18-21) points out that when the collective mobilisation aims at effecting wide-ranging and far-reaching changes in the major institutional system, comprising the whole society, we can correctly term it a "revolutionary movement". Collective mobilisation aimed at changes within a system is a "quasi-movement". The direction and rationale for such change is provided by the ideology of the movement.

Ideology, organisation, leadership, strategy and tactics are important camponents of a social movement and are closely attached to the process of collective mobilisation. Facets of these components tend to change in the course of a social movement. Sooner or later a social movement becomes subject to the process of routinisation (M.S.A. Rao 1979: 3-10; 1983: 251). Ofen a protest mcvement starts off with a radical ideology but develops its own establishment in turn. A protest movement which rejects the existing institutions will in turn attempt to codify its belief system and provide institutionalised arrangement to enforce its code of conduct. But a movement with a defined ideology, when it becomes a well-established political party, ceases to be a movement.

The ideological orientation, organisation and form of mass mobilisation are most crucial for the direction, achievement, continuity and change of a peasant movement. Celebrated peasant movements manifested themselves at particular points of time, but their legacy was carried through mass mobilisation over a period of time. New forms of mass mobilisation also emerged in the process with corresponding ideological, organisational and tactical shifts.

Against this backdrop we propose to classify peasant movements as "radical peasant movements" and "reformative peasant movements" based on the ideological orientation and the form and direction of mobilisation of the peasantry. A "radical peasant movement" is one where uninstitutionalised mass mobilisation has been initiated and guided by radical ideology for rapid social change. It is directed towards structural change in agrarian society. A "reformative peasant movement" on the other hand, is one where institutionalised mass mobilisation is initiated by recognised bodies or political parties and for gradual social change. Mobilisation here is directed to initiate change in certain selected institutional arrangements of society. Peasant movements, however, are not discretely radical or reformative: rather, one may be an extension of another over a period of time. (We shall discuss this scheme of classification in greater detail in Chapter VI.)

The socio-economic and political roles of women especially in the agrarian society, are essentially structured by age-old traditions, beliefs, values, customs and the process of socialisation. The structured roles of members of society are essentially gender based: gender plays a crucial role in shaping the ways in which men and women participate in the social, economic and political roles. Though traditioanlly rural women have been perceived as the custodians of traditions and beliefs, and their low participation in political activities has been interpreted in terms of "women's backward consciousness" or "passivity", the hidden reality is yet to be recorded. The structural arrangement of society provides women an unequal position, but while responding to the exigencies of the social need women have shown potential for struggle and resistance visibly equal to that of men. This holds largely true in the realm of women's participation in political activities and peasants' struggle.

Women's participation in political activity and mass mobilisation increases in societal crisis. Their response to such exigencies has been a strong indicator of social crisis and conflict, and has been decisive in extending the mass base of such movements.

A sociological analysis of working women's participation in peasant movements, and mass mobilisation at different stages of socio-economic formation, involves a vast array of questions: Why do women participate in peasant movements and other forms of political mobilisation? What are the socio-economic conditions that encourage or obstruct women's participation? What changes take place in the form and extent of women's participation when a "radical peasant movement" turns into a "reformative peasant movement"? Why do women differ in their response to mass mobilisation when a movement is institutionalised? What has been the nature of women's response in institutionalised mass mobilisation in terms of their economic position in the agrarian society? How are women's issues articulated by women themselves or are focused on in the process of mobilisation of the peasantry? How can the differential rates of women's participation in peasant movements at different stages of the transition of society be explained?

This study endeavours to respond to all these questions intensively and explain the major facets in women's participation in the peasant movements in terms of the relationships between the ideology of peasant movements on the one hand and the "accumulated deprivation syndrome" of the working class rural women on the other. It is formulated that within the broad ideological perspective of radical movements rural women find enormous scope to manifest their latent discontent of "accumulated deprivation syndrome". The "accumulated deprivation syndrome" denotes a social condition where women are given an extremely low position in society. The low social status both in the family and society arises out of predominance of patriarchal norms and values, and the women's own illiteracy, lack or nil access to property, poverty, economic insecurity, exploitation, unemployment, drudgery, and marginalisation. In the ideological frame of reference of reformative movements, rural women have very little scope to manifest and articulate their latent discontent. The form and extent of their participation in these movements is primarily shaped by the objective conditions of their life and the broad processes of socio-economic formations of society.

III

THE STATE AND SOCIETY

The State of West Bengal came into existence as a result of the withdrawal of the colonial power from the subcontinent, enactment of Indian Independence Act, 1947 and the partition of Bengal the same year. Since then there has been a new dynamism in the state and society of West Bengal in terms of large-scale in-migration, transfer of political power, strong political agitations, agrarian and industrial unrests, and broad socio-economic formation. All these have affected the micro and macro social processes operating both at the wider and local level of society. In Chapter I, we discussed the main facets of the agrarian transformation of West Bengal. In the following chapters, we shall discuss important dimensions of its socio-economic and political formations. With a view to laying the foundation of the study we shall describe over here some of the basic features of the state and its society in terms of demography, caste and ethnic composition and economy of the two broad regions, three districts and social structure of the four villages under study.

West Bengal, one of the constituent states of the Republic of India in the east, may be broadly divided into two natural geographical divisions, namely the Gangetic Plain and the Himalayan and sub-Himalayan zone. The upper limit of the Gangetic Plain is the northern border of West Dinajpur, which is a watershed. The Gangetic plain has numerous marshes and shallow lakes. The entire area has deep alluvial soil suitable for agriculture. The sub-Himalayan tract, known as Duars or Tarai comprising the districts of Jalpaiguri and Cooch Bihar, consists of low land. Some of the finest tea plantations of India are situated here. North of the Duars the Himalayan mountain ranges start, where the District of Darjeeling is located (EBI 1977: 786).

According to the 1981 census, the total population of the State was 54,580,647 of which 28,560,901 were males and 26,019,746 were females, giving a sex ratio of 947 females per 1,000 males. West Bengal is the fourth largest state in terms of population with the second highest density of population (615 per square kilometre) among the states in India. The Scheduled Castes constitute around 22 per cent and the Scheduled Tribes 6 per cent of the population of the state. Around 41 per cent of the population is literate and the percentages of literacy for males and females are 50.67 per cent and 30.25 per cent respectively.

Though West Bengal is one of the major industiral states in the country with around 7,500 registered working factories and 184,300 registered small scale industries, agriculture still plays a dominant role in the economy of the state, contributing nearly 50 per cent of the state income and providing 60 per cent of its employment. Gross irrigated area of the state is nearly 36 per cent of the total cultivated area. The state occupies a leading position among the rice producing states and it earns considerable foreign exchange through exports of jute and tea (Government of India 1985: 599).

Bengal has always fostered literature, art, music and drama. Bengali literature exhibited a vigorous creative activity after its first contact with the West in the early eighteenth century and ranks foremost amongst the literature of India. It has produced, among others, the Nobel Prize-winning poet Rabindranath Tagore (1861-1941). The theatre is popular in Bengal and "Yatras" and "Kavi Gans", both open air performances, are popular in the countryside. Bengali film industry has received much prominence and secured national and international awards. Rabindra Sangeet i.e., songs composed by Tagore, which draw on the pure Indian classical as well as traditional folk music exert a powerful influence in Bengali cultural life (EBI 1977: 788). The national anthems of India and Bangladesh are part of Rabindra Sangeet.

West Bengal can be divided into distinctive geo-climatic and cultural regions of north and south. North Bengal, consisting of five districts (Cooch Bihar, Jalpaiguri, Darjeeling, West Dinajpur and Malda), covers 24.62 per cent geographical area of the state. It enjoys a strategic geographic location with international borders, with Nepal in the north-west, Bhutan in the north and Bangladesh in the east. The landscape of North Bengal has distinctive Himalayan and sub-Himalayan character, though the district of Malda has the character of Gangetic Plains.

Of the total population of the state less than 18 per cent live in North

Bengal. Compared to the state and national average literacy rate is very low in this part of West Bengal. Less than 29 per cent of the popultion is literate and the literacy rates for males and females are 38 per cent and 29 per cent respectively. The Scheduled Castes and the Scheduled Tribes form a significant section of the population, 29.38 per cent and 11.29 per cent respectively.

Though tea plantation is well developed in the Darjeeling district and in the Duars areas, North Bengal has remained both industrially and agriculturally backward with a sluggish rate of urbanisation. In this part of the state only 11.44 per cent people live in urban areas, while at the state level urban population constitutes more than 26 per cent. Hence, the pressure of population has enormously increased on traditional agriculture in North Bengal as the other avenues of employment have not developed significantly. Of the total main workers of North Bengal two-thirds are engaged in agriculture.

Because of its economic backwardness and a high concentration of the Scheduled Caste and Tribal population there—who are the most exploited in the countryside—North Bengal has since long been the breeding ground of several vociferous peasant movements. The most noteworthy of these are: the Indigo Cultivators' Revolt of 1860, the Tebhaga Movement of 1946-47 and the Naxalite Movement of 1967-69.

South Bengal comprises eleven districts, namely, Murshidabad, Nadia, Hooghli, Howrah, Twenty-Four Parganas, Bankura, Purulia, Burdwan, Birbhum, Midnapur and Calcutta. This part altogether covers more than 75 per cent of the area of the state and has a typical Gangetic landscape, mostly of alluvial formation, which is suitable for rice cultivation.

More than 82 per cent of the population of the state lives in South Bengal. Its literacy rate is significantly higher than that of North Bengal and that of the state and national average. Around 46 per cent of the population of this region is literate and literacy rates for males and females are 55.3 per cent and 33.57 per cent respectively. The Scheduled Castes and the Scheduled Tribes together account for around 25 per cent of the population.

The agriculture of South Bengal is significantly developed. The irrigation facilities provided by the Damodar Valley, Mayurakshi, and Kangasabati projects and government-sponsored deep and shallow-tubewell and "river-lift" irrigation schemes have provided the farmers with ample opportunities to usher in the Green Revolution in some parts of the region. Some of its districts are agriculturally highly developed and are

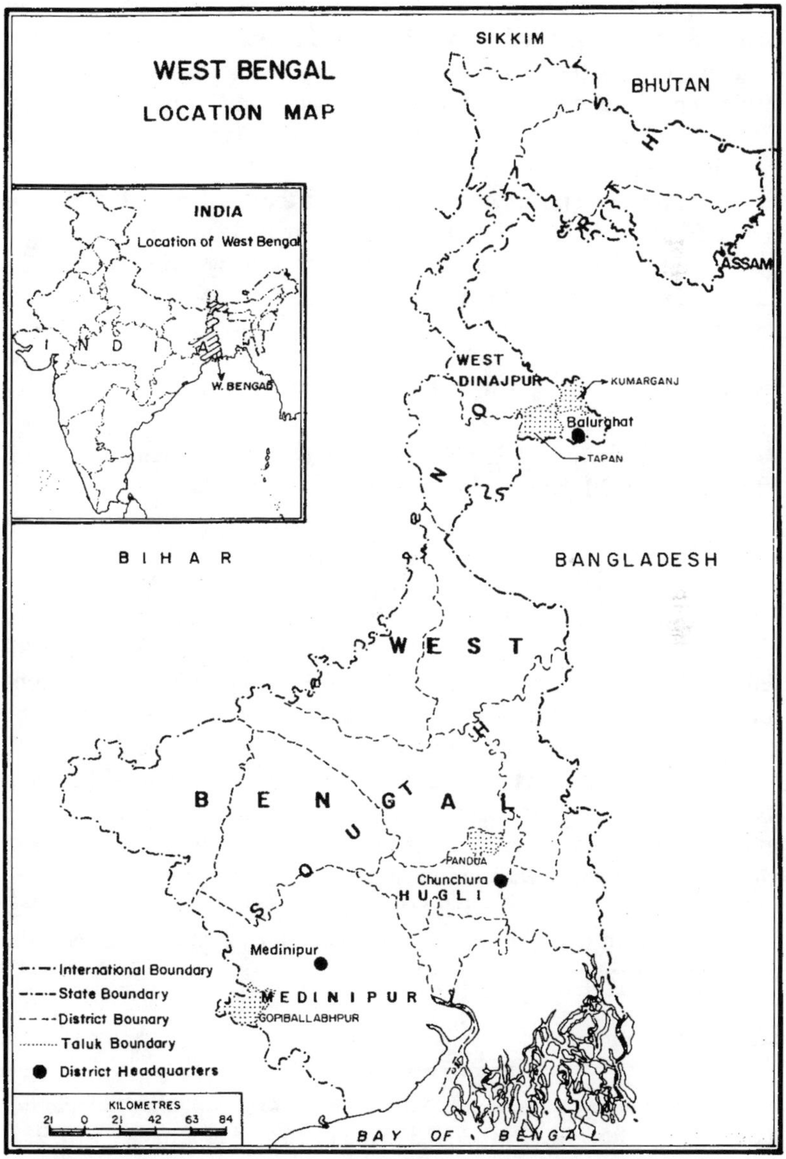

WEST BENGAL
LOCATION MAP
SIKKIM
BHUTAN
ASSAM
INDIA
Location of West Bengal
I N D I A
W. BENGAL
WEST DINAJPUR
KUMARGANJ
Balurghat
TAPAN
BIHAR
BANGLADESH
NORTH
WEST
BENGAL
SOUTH
PANDUA
Chunchura
HUGLI
Medinipur
MEDINIPUR
GOPIBALLABHPUR
International Boundary
State Boundary
District Bounary
Taluk Boundary
District Headquarters
KILOMETRES
21 0 21 42 63 84
BAY OF BENGAL

comparable to any other similar parts of Northern India. The proportion of the workers engaged in agriculture is considerably lower in this part than in North Bengal. Less than 53 per cent of the working force of South Bengal is engaged in agriculture. This part of the state is developed also in a number of manufacturing industries, of which jute mills and iron and steel industry are important. The rate of urbanisation is also considerably high in South Bengal with around 30 per cent of its population living in the urban areas.

Peasant movements which originated in the northern parts of Bengal were diffused and sustained in many parts of South Bengal. The most noteworthy of this have been the diffusion of the Tebhaga Movement in 24 Parganas, and the Naxalite Movement in Midnapur, Nadia, and in other districts.

The Districts

For greater indepth detail, three districts are studied here. These are, West Dinajpur, Midnapur and Hooghli.

West Dinajpur

According to the 1981 census, the district has 2,404,947 persons, 1,241,611 of them male and 1,163,336 female with a sex-ratio of 94 females per 100 males. The Scheduled Castes and Tribal populations together form 41 per cent of the population. Only 26.92 per cent of the population is literate and the literacy rates for males and females are 36.13 per cent and 17.08 per cent respectively. Less than 12 per cent of the population live in urban areas. The economy is predominantly based on traditional agriculture, which accounts for 75.4 per cent of employment. However, the district leads in jute and rice production in the state.

West Dinajpur has witnessed various radical peasant struggles, including the Indigo Cultivators' Revolt, Tebhaga Movement and the Naxalite Movement.

Midnapur

One of the two southernmost districts of West Bengal, Midnapur has a population of 6,742,769 (3,455,375 male, 3,247,421 female), with 95.2 females per 100 males. The Scheduled Castes and the Scheduled Tribes together form 22.6 per cent of the population. Around 43 per cent of the population is literate with 55 per cent of the males and 30 per cent of the females literate.

Though Midnapur is in the Gangetic Plains, not all of its land is cultivable. A vast area of the district is covered by small bushes and forests with high tracts of barren land. The district is backward both industrially and agriculturally and there has been an increasing pressure of population on agriculture. Of the total main workers 76.41 per cent are engaged in agriculture (76.3 per cent of the males and 78 per cent of the females) (Census of India 1981).

Midnapur has a long history of peasant participation in various movements, including the Naxalite uprising in Gopiballavpur and Debra police stations of this district in 1967-71.

Hooghli

The population is 3,557,252 (1,863,728 male, 1,693,524 female) of which 24.67 per cent is Scheduled Caste and Scheduled Tribe. Around 49 per cent of the population is literate (57.99 per cent of the males, 38.65 per cent of the females) (Census of India 1981). Around 30 per cent of the people live in the urban areas. Industrial establishments of different sizes play a key role in the economy. As non-agricultural economic activity has flourished in this district, there has been less pressure of population on agriculture. Less than 52 per cent of the main workers of the district are engaged in agriculture; and the male and female rates of work participation in agriculture are 49.86 per cent and 69.35 per cent respectively (Census of India 1981).

This district is highly agriculturally developed. With high-yielding variety, cash crop and multicrop cultivation and adoption of scientific tools and technology, Hooghli has been one of the leading districts of West Bengal.

The Villages

The Socio-economic profile of the villages under reference is presented below.

Gofanagar

Gofanagar is a multi-caste village in the jurisdiction of Tapan police station of Balurghat sub-division, West Dinajpur district. It is 16 kilometres away from Balurghat, the district headquarters. It has no systematic road or transport to Balurghat and the outside world.

Gofanagar has a population of 576 of which 308 are male and 268 female. The number of households is 120, divided among four castes and one tribal group. The Sadgope and the Baishnav belong to the upper strata of the caste hierarchy, the Karmakar and the Mallik are Scheduled Castes, while the Santals are a Scheduled Tribe.

Table 3.1: Population and Literacy by Caste in Gofanagar

Caste/ Ethnic Group	No. of House-holds	Population				Literacy			
		Male	Female	Total	Percentage of total population	Male	Female	Total	Percentage of total literate
Upper Castes	57 (47.5)*	174	141	315† (81)	54.69	158@ (90.8)	119@ (83.4)	277 (88.0)@	88.2
Scheduled Castes	38 (40.0)	92	99	191 (107.6)	33.16	21 (22.8)	2 (2.0)	23 (12.0)	7.3
Scheduled Tribes	15 (12.5)	42	28	70 (66.6)	12.15	12 (28.5)	2 (7.0)	14 (20.0)	4.5
Total	120 (100.00)	308	268	576 (87.0)	100.00	191 (62.1)	123 (45.8)	314 (54.5)	100.0

Notes: * Figures in parentheses in this column are the percentage of total population.
† Figures in parentheses in this column are the female sex ratio or number of females per 100 males.
@ Figures in parentheses in these columns are literate male, female and total persons as percentage of the respective caste/ethnic category.

Source: Intensive village survey by the author in 1985-86.

Table 3.1 shows that of the 120 households in the village 57 belong to the upper castes and 48 and 15 to the Scheduled Castes and Scheduled Tribes respectively. It needs to be noted that six upper caste and 40 Scheduled Caste households migrated to this village in the 1960s from the then East Pakistan, now Bangladesh, while there has been considerable out-migration of the tribal people because of eviction of tribal sharecroppers by the landowners.

The female sex ratio of 87 in this village is significantly lower than the state average. Among the tribals, female sex ratio is only 67. This low figure is partly explained by the fact that some of the tribals migrating out of this village, send their female member out earlier, while the male members stay back to look after the household assets. The female sex ratio among the upper and the Scheduled Castes is 81 and 107.6 respectively.

The literacy rate of this village, at 54.5 per cent, is considerably higher than the state average of 40.94 per cent. The literacy rates for males and females are 62 per cent and 45.8 per cent respectively. Literacy, however, is unevenly spread among the different caste and tribal groups. While the Scheduled Castes and the Scheduled Tribes together constitute more than 45 per cent of the population, they account for less than 12 per cent of the literates, while the upper castes who constitute less than 55 per cent of the population constitute more than 88 per cent of the literates (90.8 per cent male and 83.4 per cent female). Only 12 per cent of the Scheduled Caste and 20 per cent of the Scheduled Tribe people are literate. While the literacy rates for the Scheduled Caste and Scheduled Tribe males are 22.8 per cent and 28.5 per cent respectively, for their females these are only 2 and 7 per cent respectively.

Though the economy of Gofanagar is predominantly based on agriculture, with all the villagers attached to agriculture either directly or indirectly, the village is agriculturally backward. Only a few upper caste households own pump sets and shallow tube-wells. Mostly, traditional tools and technology are used, such as the plough driven by unhealthy bullocks. Since the early 1970s a few landowners have started using chemical fertilisers, and cultivating HYV rice, jute, potato etc., but due to lack of irrigation facilities, mechanisation in agriculture has not taken place. There also has not been any significant development in the avenues for non-agricultural economic activities.

Table 3.2 : Occupation by Caste in Gofanagar

Caste/ Ethnic Group	No. of House-holds	Primary Occupations				Secondary Occupations			
		Culti-vation	Agri-cultural Labo-urers	Ser-vice	Busi-ness and Others	Culti-vation	Agri-cultural Labo-urers	Ser-vice	Busi-ness and Others
Upper Castes	57	38	1	16	2	18	—	7	8
Scheduled Castes	48	—	48	—	—	6	—	—	—
Scheduled Tribes	15	—	15	—	—	8	—	—	1
Total	120	38	64	16	2	32	—	7	9
Per-centage	(100)	(31.7)	(53.3)	(13.4)	(1.6)				

Notes: To categorise the primary and secondary occupation of a household, occupations of all members of the household are taken into consideration. The primary occupation is identified to be that source from where the major portion of the yearly income of a household is derived. The secondary occupation is defined to be that from where its subsidiary income is derived.
The figures in parentheses are the percentages to the total number of the households.

Source: Intensive field survey by the author in 1985-86.

Table 3.2 indicates that agriculture plays a crucial role in the economic life of the villagers. Of the 120 households of the village as many as 102 (i.e., more than 85per cent) are engaged in agriculture primarily, while only 18 households are in non-agricultural occupations. Of the 48 households reported to have a secondary occupation 32 again are engaged in agriculture. So far as non-agricultural occupations are concerned, service in government or semi-government organisations and business have been undertaken by a few upper caste persons. Fifteen out of the 16 households with non-agricultural secondary occupation belong to the upper castes.

As many as 53 per cent of the households are of agricultural labourers, nearly all of them belonging to the lower castes. Out of the 57 upper caste households 38 are engaged in cultivation, 18 in service and business and only one in the category of agricultural labourer. Again, 33 households of these castes have potential sources of secondary occupation—18 in cultivation and 15 in service and business.

As against this, all the 63 Scheduled Caste and Tribal households are agricultural labourers primarily and only 14 of them have cultivation as secondary occupation. There is only one Scheduled Tribe household with a betel-shop as secondary occupation.

The salient features of village Gofanagar are, thus, as follows:

(a) Due to lack of irrigation facilities, mechanisation has not taken place in agriculture. Consequently, the village has remained agriculturally backward.

(b) As alternative avenues of employment have not emerged, only limited occupational diversification has taken place.

(c) There is a high concentration of the population in backward agriculture.

(d) In spite of agricultural backwardness, sharp inequality has emerged in terms of access over non-agricultural occupation and education and landholding (to be discussed in Chapter IV).

(e) Agrarian inequality is closely associated with the social structure of the village, especially in terms of caste and ethnicity.

Khanpur

Khanpur is a multi-caste village located 18 kilometres north-east of Balurghat, the district headquarters of West Dinajpur, and comes under the administrative jurisdiction of the Sub-division, Police Station and Development block of Balurghat. It is connected with Balurghat by a pucca road and regular bus services.

Khanpur has a population of 1,672 (876 male and 786 female) distributed over 371 households of 15 caste or ethnic groups. The Brahmin, Kayastha and Sadgope belong to the upper castes, the Mahishya and the Baishnav to the middle castes and the Mali, Yogi, Rajbansi, Polia, Colkamar, and the Chamars to the Scheduled Castes. The Santals are a Scheduled Tribe while the Mahatos are an ex-tribe. There are also a few Muslim families. The upper and the middle castes together constitute around 24 per cent of the households, the ex-tribes, Scheduled Castes and the Scheduled Tribes 73 per cent and Muslims 3 per cent (Table 3.3). While there has been considerable immigration of upper caste households to Khanpur since independence, there has also been considerable out-migration of the Tribal households after the Tebhaga Movement.

Table 3.3: Population and Literacy by Caste in Khanpur

Caste/ Ethnic Group	No. of House-holds	Population				Literacy			
		Male	Female	Total	Percentage of total population	Male	Female	Total	Percentage of total literate
Upper Castes	21 (5.7)	45	44	89 (97.8)*	5.3	39 (86.7)†	34 (77.3)†	73 (82.0)†	13.5
Middle Castes	70 (18.9)	178	150	328 (84.3)	19.6	131 (75.7)	89 (59.3)	220 (67.1)	40.0
Ex-tribes	60 (16.2)	164	149	313 (90.9)	18.7	60 (36.6)	126 (17.4)	86 (27.5)	16.0
Scheduled Castes	194 (52.3)	438	402	840 (91.8)	50.2	107 (24.2)	39 (9.7)	146 (17.4)	27.1
Scheduled Tribes	14 (3.8)	29	25	54	3.2	8	3	11 (20.4)	2.0
Muslims	12 (3.2)	22	26	48	2.9	3	—	3 (6.2)	1.0
Total	371	876	796	1672 (91.00)	-	348 (39.7)	191 (24.0)	539 (32.2)	32.2

Notes: *Figures in parentheses in this column are the female sex ratio or number of females per 100 males.

† Figures in parentheses in these columns are the percentages of their respective category.

Source: Intensive village survey by the author in 1985-86.

Female sex ratio of Khanpur is 91, which is nearly equal to the state average. In terms of caste, it is 97.8 among the upper castes, 85 among the middle castes, 90.9 among the ex-tribes and 91.8 among the Scheduled Castes. Among the Scheduled Tribes there are 25 females to 29 males and among the Muslims 26 females to 22 males.

The literacy rate in Khanpur is 32.2 per cent which is significantly lower than the state average of 40.94 per cent. The literacy rate for males is 39.7 per cent and for females 24 per cent. Caste hierarchy and literacy rate are closely correlated. Thus, the literacy rate is 82 per cent among the upper castes, 67 per cent among middle castes, 27.5 per cent among the ex-tribes, 17.4 per cent among the Scheduled Castes, 20.4 per cent among the Scheduled Tribes and 6.2 per cent among the Muslims. The upper and the middle castes, which together constitute less than 25 per cent of the population have more than 54 per cent of the literates. On the other hand, the Scheduled Castes, the Scheduled Tribes, ex-tribes and Muslims who form more than 75 per cent of the population have less than 46 per cent of the literates. The higher levels of education are found only among the upper and the middle caste groups.

Females are lagging behind in literacy across the caste/ethnic groups, with the gap between the male and female literacy rate being conspicuously sharp at the bottom of the caste hierarchy.

Khanpur receives substantial assured water supply from different sources. While water from big-ponds and shallow tube-well helps in the cultivation of rabi crops, the deep tube-wells have facilitated cultivation of HYV crops in recent years. HYV seeds, chemical fertilisers, underground water technology, pesticides, etc. have been widely introduced, but the rigorous implementation of land reform laws have discouraged the big landowners from introducing sophisticated farm mechanisation. Commodification and commercialisation of agriculture have nevertheless taken place considerably, opening up avenues of alternative economic activities both inside and outside the village.

Agriculture, however, remains the mainstay of livelihood. More than 96 per cent of the villagers are primarily engaged in agriculture. As to secondary occupations, 83.5 per cent of the villagers have a subsidiary means of livelihood, 30 per cent of them are engaged in non-agricultural economic activities such as sale and purchase of agricultural produce, betel-shop, tea-stall, cycle repairing shop, grocery, vegetable shop and business of Muri (puffed rice) and Chira (beaten rice), and service in government offices or educational institutions.

Caste and ethnic composition have close affinity with the occupational structure of the village. Of the total households primarily engaged in agriculture, more than 68 per cent are agricultural labourers and 27.8 per cent cultivators. The great majority of the agricultural labour households are from the lower strata of the caste hierarchy and from the tribal and

Muslim communities. On the other hand, 70 of the 103 cultivator households and again 13 of the 15 households engaged in service and business belong to the upper and middle caste groups. As regards secondary occupations, 32 of the 91 upper and middle caste groups have subsidiary occupations, 19 in agriculture and 13 in service and business (Table 3.4).

Table 3.4: Occupation by Caste in Khanpur

Caste/ Ethnic Group	No. of House-holds	Primary Occupations				Secondary Occupations			
		Culti-vation	Agri-cultural Labour	Ser-vice	Busi-ness	Culti-vation	Agri-cultural Labour	Ser-vice	Busi-ness
Upper Castes	21	18	1	—	2	—	—	3	6
Middle Castes	70	52	7	6	5	13	6	—	4
Ex-tribes	60	1	59	—	—	57	1	—	21
Scheduled Castes	194	29	163	—	2	115	8	—	56
Scheduled Tribes	14	—	14	—	—	11	—	—	—
Muslims	12	3	9	—	—	9	—	—	—
Total	371	103	253	6	9	205	15	3	87
Percen-tages	(100)	(22.6)	(68.2)	(1.62)	(2.42)				

Note : Percentages have been calculated in terms of the toal number of households.

Source: Intensive field survey by the author in 1985-86.

A significant segment of the ex-tribes, Scheduled Castes, Scheduled Tribes and Muslim households has cultivation as its secondary occupation. This is mainly because of the small size of landholdings among them. The small and marginal sizes of landholdings along with agricultural wage earning have not been sufficient for the subsistence of an important section of population. A considerable number of the households, mainly belonging to these caste/ethnic groups, have opted for small business as their secondary source of income.

Though agriculture remains the most important avenue of employment for women, with the changing economic scenario a significant portion of them have opted for non-agricultural activities. They have opted for business of Muri and Chira as important alternative avenues for their employment and income. The Mahato, Rajbansi and Polia women have shown sufficient enthusiasm in this venture.

The Tebhaga Movement of 1947 took place in Khanpur and this has made Khanpur an important place to visit not only for politicians but also social scientists and journalists.

The salient features of the socio-economic processes of village Khanpur are as follows:

(a) The village has been introduced to the process of rapid economic development and social change.
(b) There has been an increasing thrust for non-agricultural activities especially among the lower strata of the village. With the establishment of market and communication network in the village the scope of this thrust has increased.
(c) Women of the lower strata have taken the initiative in undertaking small business activities along with occupational diversification.
(d) The process of agricultural modernisation has been restricted to the upper and the middle castes.
(e) Caste and ethnicity are closely correlated to the economic structure and class inequality.

Panpara

Panpara is a multicaste village in the Boinchi Comprehensive Area Development Project (CADP) of Pandua police station. It is in the Sadar Sub-division of Chunchura in district Hooghli and is located contiguous to Burdwan district. Panpara is well connected with urban centres. The nearest railway station is 2 kilometres away and the National Highway 1.5 Kilometres from the village. A metalled road connects the village with Burdwan town and Calcutta metropolitan city.

Panpara comprises 15 castes or ethnic groups. The Brahmin, Kayastha, Sadgope and Ugrakatriya form the upper castes; the Teli, Tanti, Baishnav and Tambuli the middle castes; the Bouri, Kaora, Bagdi and

Handi are the Scheduled Castes, while the Santals and the Mundas are the Scheduled Tribes. The village has 148 households and 831 persons, 442 of them male and 339 female. The upper castes account for 44.6 per cent, the middle castes 15.5 per cent and the Scheduled Castes and Scheduled Tribes 39.9 per cent of the households.

The female sex-ratio in the village is only 88 which is significantly lower than the state average of 91.1. Among the middle castes, it is 75, among the upper castes 82.8, among the Scheduled Castes 91.1 and among the Scheduled Tribes 117.

Table 3.5: Population and Literacy by Caste in Panpara

Caste/ Ethnic Group	No. of Households	Population				Literacy			
		Male	Female	Total	Percentage of Total Population	Male	Female	Total	Percentage of Total Literate
Upper Castes	66 (44.6)	204	169	373 (82.8)*	44.9	154 (75.5)†	132 (78.1)†	286 (76.7)†	59.7
Middle Castes	23 (15.5)	83	62	145 (74.7)	17.4	61 (73.5)	44 (70.9)	105 (72.4)	21.9
Scheduled Castes	29 (19.6)	90	82	172 (91.1)	20.7	40 (44.6)	22 (26.8)	62 (36.0)	12.9
Scheduled Tribes	30 (20.3)	65	76	141 (116.9)	17.0	16 (24.6)	10 (13.2)	26 (18.4)	5.4
Total	148 (100)	442	389	831 (88.0)	100.0	271 (61.3)	208 (53.5)	479 (57.6)	57.6

Notes: * The figures in parentheses in this column are the female sex ratio (number of females per 100 males).
† The figures in parentheses in these columns are the percentages of literate male, female and total persons to the respective caste/ethnic groups.

Source: Intensive field survey by the author in 1985-86.

Literacy rate in Panpara is 57.6 per cent, which is significantly higher than the state average of 40 per cent. Male and female literacy rates are 61.3 per cent and 53.5 per cent respectively. The upper and the middle caste groups, constituting 62.3 per cent of the population, have a share of

82 per cent of the literates. On the other hand, the Scheduled Castes and Scheduled Tribes, while constituting around 38 per cent of the population have only about 18 per cent of the literates. Among the upper castes, middle castes, Scheduled Castes and Scheduled Tribes the literacy rates respectively are: 76.7 per cent, 72.4 per cent, 36 per cent and 18 per cent. Among the upper castes, female literacy rate is higher than the male but lower among all other caste and tribal groups.

Panpara is the nerve centre of agricultural development in this area. Many of the new crops were first introduced here and gradually diffused to the surrounding area. There are one deep tube-well, and two mini-deep tube-wells operated by the Comprehensive Area Development Project (CADP) authorities of Boinchi and a dozen privately owned shallow tube-wells providing assured water supply throughout the year. The Damodar Valley Canal supplies water to around 40 per cent of the cultivable area of this village. The villagers have adopted many modern means of cultivation including tractors, threshers, pesticides, chemical fertilisers, HYV seed, multi-crop, etc.

Non-agricultural activities both inside and around the village have sharply increased in recent years, aided by the steady expansion of transport and market facilities. These activities have become important avenues of employment for a section of female agricultural labourers who have been displaced from agriculture due to mechanisation. While agriculture provides primary employment to 72.3 per cent of the households, 27.7 per cent are in non-agricultural activities primarily. As many as 104 households (70.3 per cent) have secondary occupations, 53 per cent of them in the non-agricultural sector and 47 per cent in the agricultural sector (Table 3.6). Businesses of different sorts have emerged as important avenues of economic activities. These include business requiring substantial capital investment like transport, large-scale sale and purchase of agricultural produce, installation of paddy husking machines, etc., and petty business like paddy husking, betel shop and tea stall, preparation of Chira and Muri (beaten rice and puffed rice), etc.

Table 3.6 : Occupation by Caste in Panpara

Caste/ Ethnic Group	No. of House-holds	Primary Occupations				Secondary Occupations			
		Culti-vation	Agri-cultural Labour	Ser-vice	Busi-ness	Culti-vation	Agri-cultural Labour	Ser-vice	Busi-ness
Upper Castes	66	40	5	12	9	20	—	—	26
Middle Castes	23	3	2	—	18	12	—	2	3
Scheduled Castes	29	—	27	—	2	1	3	—	14
Scheduled Tribes	30	1	29	—	—	13	—	—	18
Total	148	44	63	12	29	46	3	2	53
Percentages	100	29.7	42.6	8.1	19.6	44.2	2.9	1.9	5.8

Notes : Percentage has been calculated in terms of the total number of households in the primary and secondary occupations respectively.

Source : Intensive field survey by the author in 1985-86.

Agricultural development has sharpened the occupational and class inequality in the village. Of the 44 households, primarily engaged in cultivation, an overwhelming 43 are from the upper and middle castes, and only one from the Scheduled Tribe. Again, all the 12 households with service and 27 of the 29 households with business as their primary occupation are from the upper and middle castes, the remaining two being Scheduled Castes, the latter with meagre capital investment. On the other hand, 56 of the 63 agricultural labour households belong to the Scheduled Castes and Tribes.

Households with service and/or business as their primary occupation have adopted agriculture as their secondary occupation. Of the 53 households with business as secondary occupation, 29 are from the upper and middle castes and the remaining 24 from the Scheduled Castes and Scheduled Tribes.

The salient socio-economic features of Panpara, thus, are as follows:

(a) The village has been introduced to rapid economic development.
(b) Intensive and mechanised agriculture has been introduced widely.
(c) The agricultural production process has become highly profit-oriented and commercialised.
(d) A high degree of occupational diversification has taken place.
(e) Economic inequality has been sharpened in the process of agricultural and economic development which corresponds with caste and ethnic line.
(f) The upper and middle castes have been highly benefited by the development processes.
(g) The upper and middle castes have accepted business as the potential avenue of investment and maximisation of their profit, while the lower caste groups have accepted business as an alternative avenue of employment and income for subsistence.
(h) With a high degree of mechanisation and maximum use of land resources, a section of female agricultural workers has been displaced from agriculture.
(i) The village has developed an urban nexus resulting in rapid social change.

Shalgeriya

Shalgeriya is a small and predominantly tribal village located within the jurisdiction of the Police Station and Development Block of Gopiballavpur in the Jhargram Sub-division of Midnapur district. The nearest town is Jhargram 46 kilometres away. There is no systematic communication between the two. There is a metalled road which is the only communication link between the village and Police Station 8 kilometres away.

There are altogether 551 persons in Shalgeriya (288 male and 263 female) distributed over 107 households and four caste or ethnic groups — 4 Kayastha, 32 Thantari and 77 Santal and Bhumij. The Kayasthas are upper caste, the Thantaris Scheduled Caste, and the Santals and Bhumij Scheduled Tribes.

The female sex ratio at 91.3 is far below the district average of 95.1. The figure among the Scheduled Tribes is 86.9, and among the Scheduled Castes 106. There are 7 females to 8 males among the upper castes. Only

10.8 per cent of the population is literate with negligible female literacy (3 per cent) while 18 per cent of the males are literate. The Scheduled Castes have no literate female, while the Scheduled Tribes have 2 out of 185 females literate. Among the upper castes, all the females are literate.

Shalgeriya has dry, unfertile land, with only its lower portion cultivable. Of the total land area of 486 acres of the village 166 acres are under forest and another 90 acres are not available for cultivation. Till the mid-1960s the village was surrounded by deep forest. In the process of rapid deforestation evergreen trees have disappeared from the vicinity of the village.

Agriculturally Shalgeriya is very backward. It has no irrigation facility and depends on traditional tools and technology. The scope of alternative economic activities is very limited, which increases the pressure of the population on agriculture. This has led to large-scale seasonal out-migration of the agricultural work force to the agriculturally developed neighbouring districts. Though the government has distributed surplus

Table 3.7 : Population and Literacy by Caste in Shalgeriya

Caste/ Ethnic Group	No. of Households	Population				Literacy			
		Male	Female	Total	Percentage of Total Population	Male	Female	Total	Percentage of Total Literate
Upper Castes	4 (3.7)	8	7	15	2.73	5	7	12	20.00
Scheduled Castes	32 (30.0)	67	71	138 (106.0)*	25.04	8 (11.9)†	—	8 (5.8)†	13.3
Scheduled Tribes	71 (66.3)	213	185	398 (86.9)	72.23	38 (17.8)	2 (1.1)†	40 (10.1)	66.7
Total	107 (100)	288	263	551 (91.3)	100.00	51 (17.7)	9 (3.2)	60 (10.8)	100.00

Notes : * Figures within the parentheses in this column are the female sex ratio (number of females per 100 males).

† The figures in parentheses in these columns are the percentages of literate male, female and total persons to the respective category.

Source: Intensive field survey by the author in 1985-86.

vested land among the villagers, poverty has not declined. Poverty, unemployment, seasonal out-migration, and uncertainty are endemic in Shalgeriya, especially for the Scheduled Castes and Tribes. All these are reflected in the occupational structure of the village. Table 3.8 shows that 98.2 per cent of the households of the village are primarily engaged in agriculture and 93.5 per cent of the households are of agricultural labourers primarily. There are 49 households with secondary occupation of which 29 are again in agriculture.

Table 3.8 : Occupation by Caste in Shalgeriya

Caste/ Ethnic Group	No. of House-holds	Primary Occupations				Secondary Occupations			
		Culti-vation	Agri-cultural Labour	Ser-vice	Busi-ness	Culti-vation	Agri-cultural Labour	Ser-vice	Busi-ness
Upper Castes	4	2	—	2	—	2	—	—	—
Scheduled Castes	32	—	32	—	—	—	—	—	20
Scheduled Tribes	71	3	68	—	—	27	—	—	—
Total	107	5	100	2	—	29	—	—	20
Percen-tages	100	4.7	93.5	1.8					

Note : Percentage has been calculated in terms of the total number of households.

Source : Intensive field survey by the author in 1985-86.

For most of the Scheduled Caste and Tribe households, agricultural wage earning is the primary occupation. Since they cannot produce enough from their own land they consider cultivation as the secondary source of their income. They are, however, 20 Scheduled Caste households with small business of old utensils etc. as their secondary occupation. They have no market facilities in the village and are in business only seasonally.

Of the four upper caste households in the village two are in cultivation and another two in service primarily. Two of the households have cultivation also as secondary occupation.

Shalgeriya has a distinctive historical background of participation in the Naxalite Movement. The Scheduled Caste and Scheduled Tribe population took part in all phases of the movement. Indeed, it was from Shalgeriya that the Naxalite Movement started in Gopiballavpur under the leadership of Santosh Rana and Ashim Chatterjee.

The major socio-economic processes of this village reveal that:

(a) The village has remained backward economically.
(b) The traditional tools and technology of cultivation are predominantly used.
(c) In course of deforestation population pressure on agriculture has increased enormously.
(d) There has not been any new avenue for alternative economic activity.
(e) For subsistence the Scheduled Caste and Scheduled Tribe population resort to seasonal out-migration on a large scale.
(f) The village has not been able to get over its isolation of market and institutional facilities.

IV

RURAL WOMEN IN THE TEBHAGA AND NAXALITE MOVEMENTS

Women's participation in a movement is a measure of the depth of the movement among the masses and concern of women about social issues.

> The extent and form of women's participation is indicative of characteristics of a movement as a whole. The greater the mass base of a movement, the greater women's participation and more successful the movement. Movements which are both radical and democratic have recorded the greatest success in organising women (Basu 1981: 217).

More important, women's participation offers a new dimension in the process of mobilisation. As Gandhi said :

> When women, whom we call *abala* becomes *sabala*, all those who are helpless will become powerful (Gandhi 1936: 165).

West Bengal witnessed two historic peasant movements in this century, namely the Tebhaga Movement of 1946-47 and the Naxalite Movement of 1967-71. In both, women were in the forefront of the struggle with the police, in forcible harvesting of the crops, in the meetings and campaigning and organising activities, in supplying food and maintaining communication network among the underground activists and in stimulating the moral strength for resistance.

The present chapter examines this unique phenomenon. After examining the background and the socio-economic contexts in which the peasant movements emerged, it describes the whole gamut of the peasant uprising in the selected villages and analyses the specific roles played by the women in these movements.

Tebhaga Movement (1946-47)

In 1946, on the eve of independence and partition of Bengal, a fierce peasant uprising, widely known as Tebhaga Andolan, surfaced in the United Province of Bengal. It was a movement of the sharecroppers to retain two-thirds share of the produce for themselves and thereby to reduce from one-half to one-third of the produce the rent paid to Jotedars—a class of rich farmers who held superior rights in land (Dhanagare 1976: 360). Tebhaga (two-thirds of the share) was a popular demand of the sharecroppers which was endorsed by the Bengal Kisan Sabha and recommended by the Land Revenue Commission, 1940 (Sen 1979: 443). This movement grew under the leadership of the Bengal Kisan Sabha and in the process of mobilisation agricultural labourers, sharecroppers and poor peasants in the form of tenants of various categories, became the driving force against the Jotedars, Zamindars, money-lenders, traders and the British bureaucracy. Essentially an economic struggle, the movement took a political form when it had to confront the Jotedars and the political apparatus of the state (Desai 1979: 419). From the outset women of the lowest section of the agrarian society were mobilised in the movement, and women's participation surpassed that of men after the men were arrested and the struggle intensified (Basu 1981: 221).

Background of Political Mobilisation. The Tebhaga Movement, though it was formally launched in November 1946 under the auspices of the Bengal Kisan Sabha, was the outcome of a long period of struggle. Throughout the British rule the peasantry of Bengal had experienced a steady decline in their economic position. In the early twentieth century this process was precipitated with the extreme growth of uneconomic holdings and subinfeudation of landownership, on the one hand, and increasing burden of indebtedness, extra-economic coercion, tenurial insecurity, rack-renting and poverty of the peasantry in the lower strata, on the other, these two processes being mutually intertwined.

In the 1930s, there was a sharp increase in the transfer of occupancy rights and a tremendous rise in the sharecropping system of land cultivation. The number of the transfer of occupancy rights, which was 85,361 in

1929 had more than trebled to 295,371 in 1936 (Haque 1939: 311). These land transfers had serious implications to the agrarian relations of that period because they brought into the hands of commercialised non-cultivating owners a considerable amount of land. A distinctly new category of landowners thus came into being with substantial permanent and transferable occupancy rights on land in the countryside of Bengal (Chattopadhyay 1981: 125). Known as *Jotedars*, this category interposed itself between the actual cultivator and the landlord leading to the decay of poor peasants and medium cultivators. The *Jotedars* practised large-scale traditional farming employing either sharecroppers (known as *Adhiars* or *Bargadars*) or agricultural labourers (Ghosh and Dutta 1977: 62-63). In North Bengal the Jotedars were socially supreme; they possessed thousands of acres of land and got these cultivated by the Scheduled Caste and Scheduled Tribe sharecroppers and agricultural labourers.

A significant portion of the poor peasants who lost their lands to the Jotedars because of their debt, mortgage and distress sale, were resettled on the same land as sharecroppers (for details see Chapter I). Regarding their status in the rural society the Land Revenue Commission wrote in 1940:

> The rapid increase in the number of the bargadars is one of the most disquieting features of the present times; and it is an indication of the extent to which hereditary raiyots are losing their status and being depressed to a lower standard of living. It is true that the successive provisions of the Tenancy Acts have endowed the raiyots with the practical ownership of their land. But a large and increasing proportion of the acutal cultivators have no part of the elements of ownership, no protection against excessive rent and no security of tenure... (LRC 1940, Vol. 1: 38-39).

Questions pertaining to the deteriorating economic condition of the peasantry of Bengal surfaced time and again during the British rule. But it was only in the 1920s and onward that these questions received systematic focus. In this period the left forces also were seeking to organise the peasantry in Bengal. In 1920 the foundation of Indian Communist movement was laid at the second Congress of the Communist International in Moscow and the Central Committee of the Communist Party of India was formed in December 1925. But the Communist movement went underground in the wake of the Kanpur Conspiracy case (1923-24) in which leaders of the Communist Party of India were accused of conspiring against the State. To continue the party's work, under the instruction of M.N. Roy, the leading Marxist and the founding member of the Communist party of India, the Workers and Peasants' Party (WPP) was formed. The WPP stood for complete independence based on social and economic emancipation, demanded nationalisation of industries, services and land. The WPP, however, was more involved in organising the urban and industrial workers than in mobilising the peasantry. The Krishak Praja Party (KPP) formed in 1929, emerged as an important political party in the 1930s to plead for the abolition of the *Zamindari* system, and establishment of peasant proprietorship in land. The KPP had communal orientation, drawing its main support from the poor peasantry of the Muslim community, but in alliance with the Congress it formed the first popular Ministry in Bengal and subsequently appointed the Land Revenue Commission in 1938 (Dhanagare 1976: 366-68).

Meanwhile, when the Communist Party was banned in 1934 and many of the Communist workers were arrested, a significant number of them went to the remote rural areas to evade arrest. They started secretly mobilising the rural poor on local issues. Their work received a fillip with the formation of the Bengal Kisan Sabha in 1936, a provincial branch of the All India Kisan Sabha. The main objectives of the Kisan Sabha were to secure complete freedom of the peasantry from economic exploitation and attain complete economic and political power for the peasants and workers and for all other exploited classes (Rasul 1976: 5). Gradually, Kisan Sabha workers became active in organising the peasants and workers against the tyranny of the big landowners. These activists also started bringing the exploited rural peasantry under the organisational set-up of the Kisan Sabha.

The Kisan Sabha began to radicalise its agrarian programme in the late 1930s after the Krishak Praja Party made a volte-face on agrarian problems, and rather than fulfilling its pre-election promise of abolishing the Zamindari system, began to openly defend it (Dhanagare 1976: 369). The Bengal Kisan Sabha on the other hand continued to push the agrarian issue. It submitted a memorandum to the Land Revenue Commission in November 1938 pleading for the "abolition of Zamindari" and demanded "peasant ownership" (Sen 1979: 435).

In these circumstances the Report of the Land Revenue Commission became a landmark in the history of agrarian dynamics in Bengal. The Commission recommended in 1940 that :

> all bargadars should be treated as tenants, that the share of the crops legally recoverable from them should be one-third, instead of half

(Vol. I, 1940: 69).

But circumstances were not conducive to implementing this recommendation. The agrarian economy of Bengal, which had been recovering from the depression of 1929, once again was ravaged by the famine of 1943 which claimed millions of lives. There were successive crop failures from 1938-39 to 1942-43. The natural calamities of floods, famine and disease were also enormous from 1941 to 1945. Simultaneously, the economic condition of Bargadars worsened significantly because despite famine and other natural disasters they had to fulfil their obligation of surrendering half of their produce to the landowners. When natural disasters struck the hapless peasants the Kisan Sabha workers who were released from jail, engaged themselves in massive relief work, which brought them in close contact with the peasantry. They took this opportunity to mobilise the tenants and the Bargadars and stop them from paying rents or share of crops to the landowners (Dhanagare 1976: 166-69).

In November 1946 the Kisan Sabha passed a resolution in Calcutta for "Tebhaga" to the sharecropper. Its activists spread in the rural areas to organise the sharecroppers against the big landlords. Their activity was mainly focused in Northern Bengal, with its high incidence of sharecropping and its majority of Scheduled Caste and Tribal population especially in Dinajpur district.

The political mobilisation of the peasantry closely involved the mobilisation of peasant women as well. In the 1940s the Mahila Atmaraksha Samiti (MARS— Women Self Protection Society) was formed under the auspices of the women workers of the Communist Party. The MARS undertook relief work among the poor women, rural and urban, and among famine victims. It also contributed to the growing awareness among rural women about their rights, and to the growth of political consciousness. It mobilised peasants, workers and middle class women (Sen 1985: 198). But, this organisation was not built on class leadership. Its cadres mostly hailed from middle class or better-off peasant families (Custers 1986: 101).

Kisan Sabha Movement in Dinajpur District. Dinajpur was one of the big Zamindaris of Bengal. In 1939-40, the district had witnessed the discontent of the sharecroppers against the Jotedars in the form of the short-lived *Bhag Chasi* (Sharecroppers) Movement which, however, was defeated. The simmering discontent provided a fertile ground for Kisan Sabha activities which had held its first session at Bankura of Dinajpur district in March 1937. Sabha activists kept on organising the peasantry uninterruptedly against the Jotedars there. As their message began to spread, the poor peasants and the sharecroppers joined in as the Kisan Sabha was the hope of future for them. In 1942 the ban on the Communist Party was lifted and its leading functionaries surfaced. During the famine of 1943, while organising relief work in the district Kisan Sabha workers also organised the poverty-stricken peasantry for Tebhaga. The Sabha workers and the peasantry were further encouraged by certain political developments in the area. They felt a sense of victory when in 1946 Rupnarayan, a Rajbansi peasant, was elected to the Legislative Assembly supported by the Kisan Sabha (Sen 1979: 434-39). The Sabha had started to make an effective political intervention, and the base started spreading in the villages.

Agrarian Social Structure of Khanpur on the Eve of the Tebhaga Movement. Khanpur was a remote and predominantly agricultural village. The "aman" variety (Kharif) paddy was the only major crop cultivated. The Scheduled Castes (Rajbansi, Polia, Colkamar and Mali), the Scheduled Tribes (the Santal) and ex-tribe (Mahato) comprised the bulk of the village population and the lower stratum of the caste hierarchy. The Brahmin and the Kayastha formed the upper stratum and the Mahishya and the Baishnav the middle stratum of the caste hierarchy. There were also a few Muslim families.

Under the Zamindari system, there developed a series of intermediaries such as the Naib and the Jotedar. In the other class were the Ryots (cultivating peasants), the Bhagchasi, or Adhiars (sharecroppers) and the Khet Majur (agricultural labourers). The Naib, popularly also known as the Zamindar in the village, was at the top of the agrarian hierarchy. Indeed, the Naib was the deputy or representative of the Zamindar placed in charge of the whole or a part of the Zamindari or estate with a view to its general management (Hunter 1973: 48). The Naib and the Jotedars socially belonged to the upper castes and controlled most of the village lands. Being, also the money-lenders, they took advantage of the poverty of the Ryots and gradually appropriated most of their lands in lieu of outstanding debts or mortgage.

Table 4.1: Agrarian Classes and Castes of Khanpur on the eve of the Tebhaga Movement

Agrarian Class	Caste/Ethnic Group	Percentage of Households
1. Class of Intermediaries (Naib and Jotedars)	Upper Castes	6%
2. Cultivating Peasants (Ryots)	Mahishya, Baishnav Mahato, Rajbansi, Polia, Muslim	30%
3. Sharecroppers (Bhagchasi or Adhiars)	Santal, Mahato Rajbansi, Colkamar, Polia	46%
4. Landless Agricul-tural Labourers (Khet Majur)	Santal, Rajbansi, Colkamar, Polia, Mali, Muslims	18%

Note: The percentage of the household belonging to each agrarian class may vary marginally.

Sources: Data supplied by the villagers and old land record of the village.

Table 4.1 shows that Ryots, Bhagchasis and Khet Majurs comprised 94 per cent of the population. There was significant interchangeability among these three agrarian categories, these being small cultivators-cum-sharecroppers, small cultivators-cum-sharecroppers-cum-agricultural labourers, sharecroppers-cum-agricultural labourers and small cultivators-cum-agricultural labourers.

The class of intermediaries, constituting only 6 per cent of the households, are reported to have controlled more than 76 per cent of the cultivable land. They also had regular access and links with the administrative apparatus of the state. They cultivated their land by employing either sharecroppers or agricultural labourers. There was less risk in the sharecropping system since it gave a high amount of assured rent from the land without regular investment.

Under the sharecropping system 50 per cent of the gross produce was given to the landowners while most of the costs of production were met by the sharecroppers themselves. Customarily in the harvesting season the produced crops were stacked in the courtyard of the landowners and were threshed in their presence. The sharecroppers were given consumption loan in kind at 100 per cent rate of interest for six months. As the sharecroppers were to give 50 per cent of the produce as share to the landowners, and another significant portion of their own share as repayment of loan, they were virtually left with a very small amount of paddy. They were forced to resort to loans again on similar conditions imposed on them by the landowners. They were thus caught in a vicious circle of indebtedness to the landowners and were thus virtually dependent on them.

There was, besides, tenurial insecurity. The landowners favoured yearly settlement with the sharecroppers, terminating and employing sharecroppers as it suited them. To keep the tenure of their sharecropping secured the sharecroppers were forced to maintain certain economic and extra economic obligations with the landowners. They were as follows:

(a) They were to plough with their own cattle some plots of the landowners without receiving any payment.
(b) They were to make themselves available in the house of the landowners for any need at any time.
(c) They were to guard the life and property of the landowners without receiving any remuneration.
(d) They were not allowed to use colourful dresses, cycle or even umbrella in the presence of the landowners as a mark of respect to the latter.
(e) They were to work under *Begar* (work without wages, receiving only food) in the landowners field in the peak seasons of agricultural operation.
(f) They were to consider the landowner as the '*Annadata*' (food giver) and show him respect in every sphere of life.
(g) They were made to give false witness in the court of law to save the interest of the landowners.

In course of time, the sharecropping system, which broadly formed the backbone of the agrarian social structure became more exploitative and coercive in nature. The big landowners used this institution as a mechanism to maximise their economic interest, exercise control over a large number of population and make their social position firm and infallible. The sharecroppers on the other hand could only accept this institution with its conditions as the mainstay of their subsistence.

The Working Class Women. The working women of village Khanpur were drawn from the socially and economically backward section of society. Women from the Mahato Colkamar and Santal caste/tribal groups worked in the field both as agricultural labourers and household farm workers. Few Rajbansi and Polia women worked on their own fields. The Mali women worked as maidservants. Extra-mural activities were taboo for other women of the village. The working women were from among the class of small cultivators, sharecroppers and agricultural labourers.

Female agricultural labourers emerged as a distinctive agrarian category as the economic condition of the sharecroppers, poor peasants and agricultural labour households deteriorated. More women were forced to take up daily work on the farms for subsistence. They were low paid, subjected to sex-based wage discrimination and were made to work without specified time schedule. They had been taking advance loan under the *Dadan* system and were thus caught in a beck-and-call relationship with the landowners. Under the *Dadan* system a woman took advance loan from the landowner in kind in the lean period of the agricultural cycle on condition that she would be obliged to work for him in the peak season at the stipulated wage of the lean season.

The female agricultural labourers of the sharecropper families played an important role in maintaining tenurial security by making themselves available for the service of the female members of the landlords family. In the peak season they worked under *Begar*. They jointly shared with their husbands or any other male member of the family the burden of economic and extra-economic coercion of the landlords.

Tebhaga Struggle at Khanpur and Women's Response. Languishing under such a system heavily loaded against them, some members of the lower strata of the peasantry had individually offered resistance, only to be ruthlessly suppressed by the all-powerful Jotedars. When, therefore, the message of Tebhaga reached them as promise of better share of the fruit of their hard labour and of security, the subjugated peasantry joined the movement with many a hope.

A clandestine effort to mobilise the peasantry against the big landowners had been going on at Khanpur since the early 1940s. After the Calcutta resolution of the Kisan Sabha on Tebhaga in November 1946, Khanpur became a centre point of Kisan Sabha activities. Local Kisan Sabha workers started mobilising the sharecroppers against the big landowners of the village with the initiative and guidance of leaders working at district and state levels. They organised meetings of the sharecroppers and poor peasants. The sharecroppers were mobilised from November 1946 itself.

By and by, the sharecroppers of the village began attending open meetings of the Kisan Sabha workers organised in the village and in the neighbouring villages. The tranquillity of the villagers was broken by the new awakening, and slogans began to be heard such as "Inquilab Zindabad", "Nij *Kolane* Dhan Tolo" (Stack paddy in your own courtyard), "Langal jar jamintar" (The land belongs to the tiller), "Tebhaga Chai" (We want two-thirds of the share), "Britisher Dalal Bharat Charo" (Quit India, you agents of the British), "Hindustan Zindabad".

The newfound enthusiasm touched even the most backward women of the village. Brave kisan women took the lead in propaganda work, and often led the men in the fight, facing the hirelings of the Jotedars (Chakravarty 1980:87).

When the movement began, the Kisan Sabha activists met the villagers in the houses of the sharecroppers and poor peasants. They met in small groups, secretly and at night. The women of the household looked after the comfort of the activists, supplying them *Bidis*, *Hukka*, betal and water, etc. and prepared meals for them. Many spent hours waiting till late night for their husbands to return from the meetings. Women sheltered Kisan Sabha activists who were evading police arrest and carried messages for them.

When the movement escalated to mass action, the sharecroppers began to harvest paddy and carry it to their own '*Kholan*" (courtyard) under the instruction of the local leaders. Women cut and carried the paddy to their own courtyard defying the landowners, including even the Rajbansi and Polia women, who customarily did not work in the field. They armed themselves with bows and arrows and other lethal weapons as a precautionary measure. As the women, who had only suffered pangs of hunger, and had seen their children famished during famine, saw the golden paddy brought into their yards, they became the firmest supporters of Tebhaga (Chakravarty 1980: 90).

The harvested paddy could not, however, be threshed without the presence and consent of the landowners since the legal aspect of the share of produced crop began from this operation. But the landowners merely remained silent, playing for time. The harvested paddy remained stacked in the courtyards of the sharecroppers for more than a month, while a tense calm pervaded the village. The miseries of the sharecroppers and agricultural labour household were meanwhile increasing since agricultural activities had come to a halt. The sharecroppers were in urgent need of paddy to quench their hunger.

The event that sparked off the agitation then took place. The grazing bullock of a sharecropper entered the courtyard of the Zamindar who also happened to be a powerful man of the village. The Zamindar ordered his Barkandaj (arm-man) to impound the bullock at the police station. The news spread like wildfire. When the Barkandaj was coming out of the courtyard of the landowner with the bullock, the organised sharecroppers snatched away the bullock from him. The peasant women who had gathered in large numbers started rebuking the landowners. The incited sharecroppers then beat up the Barkandaj until he bled. Jhari Col, a woman onlooker, urged them to cut his ears and nose, though this was not done. Recalling the incident, a Colkamar woman of 60 said :

> We were feeling the pleasure of beating the landowner who had twice beaten my husband accusing him of being a thief. We were hungry, our lands were appropriated by him. We were reduced to being hungry street-dogs moving about. It was time to bite. As our people hit the Barkandaj, we vicariously felt that we were belabouring the landowner.

The incident took place on February 19, 1947. The same day the landowner lodged an FIR at the Balurghat police station implicating seventeen sharecroppers. Anticipating police action against them, the Kisan Sabha organised on open meeting at Patiram, 6 kilometres from Khanpur, the same afternoon. Addressing a well-attended meeting they blamed the landowners of Khanpur for the miseries of the poor and instructed the sharecroppers and poor peasants to remain united against the threat and oppression of the landowners-police combine.

Thus inspired, the villagers returned home ready for any eventuality. Courage had infused the downtrodden breasts, and the village that evening was the scene of unprecedented lusty slogan shouting by both men and women. "Inquilab Zindabad", they chanted, "Tebhaga Cahi". "Britisher Dalal Nipat Jak" (Let the agent of the British wither); "Jiban Jak, Tebhaga Thak" (Tebhaga even at the cost of life); "Kather Banduk fote na" (Wooden guns do not shoot). Through the listless might they prepared for the next day, the women gathering all the traditional weapons and other instruments for an innovative alarm system among the villagers. Many of them worshipped goddess Kali and Manasa praying for strength.

As expected, the police arrived the next morning. They came with a van and a truck, and arrested a few sharecroppers. This news spread like a wildfire all over the village. The Santal women of the village sounded the alarm by beating drums. The Rajbansi, Colkamar and Mahato women took it up by blowing conchshells and beating gongs and utensils. House to house the sound of the alarm spread, going from hamlet to hamlet, the village and its environs reverberating to the sounds of drums, tin jars, gongs and conchshells.

Taking their cue, a vast mass of poor peasants and sharecroppers both from Khanpur and neighbouring villages surged on the Cutcheries of the landowner where the arrested sharecroppers had been detained, appearing there with their traditional weapons like bows and arrows, lathis and axes. The women emerged at the forefront armed with lathis, broomsticks and *Kanrols* (paddy-husking pestles), *Boti* (vegetable cutter) and axes. Standing in the way of the police van they declared that they would protect their colleagues even at the cost of their lives: "Hamara morey jamo, Kintu hamar manush leya jate demona" (We will die but we will not allow our people to be taken away). They dig a ditch on the road to stop the vehicles from leaving.

Josodha Barmani, whose husband the police were taking away, attacked the police van with her axe. Other women joined her in the attack. With bows and arrows, lathis, broomsticks, axes, stones, etc. the surging mass attacked the police vehicles, while many women lay down in front of the moving vehicles. The police after giving some dire warnings to disperse, resorted to fire. The van ran over Josodha who was six months pregnant; she died on the spot. Blinded by fury, the seething mass attacked the police vehicles disregarding all notions of safety. Altogether 119 rounds were fired by the police which claimed the lives of 17 sharecroppers including two women, Josodha Burmani and Kaushalya Kamani and injured hundreds. The police beat up the injured mercilessly and even snatched away the clothes from the injured and hiding women. Additional police forces were deployed in the village the same day. They started a house-to-house search to apprehend the sharecroppers, ransacking many houses, and asking people, even women, to strip, to verify if they had any injuries that would incriminate them. A 62-year-old Rajbansi woman narrates:

> Since curfew was imposed in the village we were afraid to go out of our house. I was anxiously waiting for my son to be back. My husband was ill. A few policemen entered our house. They searched most parts of our house. The police thought that my husband was pretending illness. They dragged him and forced him to be naked. They also compelled me to show my bare arms and knees....

She recalls the events that later overtook the village:

> We were ready to face all situations, to protect ourselves from any eventuality. My husband and myself took part in all phases of the movement. We attacked the police on the day of the arrest. Even after taking the lives of 20 of our people the landowners did not feel happy. They continued to torture us with the help of the police. The police came to the village with the sole purpose of harassing and torturing us. My husband left the village. The police snatched away all our stacked paddy and even destroyed our hut. I tried to prevent them but they beat me and took the clothes off my body.
>
> The Kisan Sabha workers were visiting the village secretly. I used to take messages from them to my husband who had gone underground in the neighbouring villages. After a few days he was arrested. So were most of the others who had gone underground. While arresting the men, the police did not fail to torture them. We witnessed these things from inside the house and could only cry helplessly. I felt revengeful. Many a time I rebuked the policemen. Many women were coming to sleep in my house in the night as their husbands had also been arrested by the police. They were days of humiliation, torture, uncertainty and starvation. In spite of all these I protected my three children. My husband came back from jail after one year.

Amidst the repressive measures let loose by the landowners and the police the communication linkages among the leaders, activists and the followers broke down totally. In the absence of proper linkage and guidance on the one hand and the increasing torture of the police on the other, a slough of despond descended on the peasantry. Sharecroppers were arrested indiscriminately. The landowner with the help of the police took possession of all paddy stacked in the courtyard of the sharecroppers, denying them any share in the produce for that year, and filed criminal cases against many of them. The menfolk left the village, many of them settling in other districts. A veteran Kisan Sabha leader was jailed from 1948 to 1956 (Sen 1985: 208).

The women came forward to look after the forlorn families, to feed the children, to take care of the cattle and other dependants and to maintain the communication network among the Kisan Sabha activists and the sharecroppers who had gone underground. The women were also organised for self-protection in the absence of the male members of the family. To protect their chastity from predatory policemen they threw chilly powder mixed with sand on them. They kept themselves ready to combat any unexpected events.

The Tebhaga struggle came to an end at Khanpur without any immediate result. The bloodshed, death and torture the sharecroppers and poor peasants and their families underwent seemed to have been in vain. Many village-level activists surrendered to the landowners to avoid police torture and to protect their family and property.

Political happenings at a wider level of society then overshadowed the image and the ideology of the Tebhaga Movement, especially the attainment of Independence, partition of Bengal and the formation of the national government at the Centre and in the state of West Bengal. The ideas on land reform which were generated in the years of the Tebhaga Movement were however incorporated after a long struggle in the land reform policies of post-independence West Bengal.

Naxalite Movement 1967-1971

Till the 1960s, a gap remained in West Bengal between the land reform programmes of the state and its implementation (For details see Chapter I). The aspirations and expectations of the Tebhaga Movement still remained unfulfilled. Conditions thus gave rise to the outburst of what came to be known as the Naxalite Movement in West Bengal. Women again took an active part in all phases of this movement.

The period between 1947 and 1967 in Bengal was marked by the emergence of a series of interrelated social and political processes both at the micro and macro levels of society. Significantly, most of these social processes adversely affected the lowest section of the agrarian population. As a result of the partition of Bengal there had been a large-scale migration of Hindu population from the then East Pakistan (now Bangladesh) and this resulted in a heavy pressure of population on the backward agriculture of West Bengal. With the enactment of various land reform laws the intermediary system was legally abolished, ceiling restrictions on landholdings were imposed, provisions were made for the distribution of surplus vested land and 60 per cent of the produced share to the sharecroppers, but in reality the significant laws remained unknown to the intended beneficiaries. In the existing gap between the enactment of land reform laws and their implementation, the unscrupulous big landowners took recourse to mala-fide land transfer. Eviction of sharecroppers went on unhindered. The notified surplus vested land remained in possession of the big landowners. All these resulted in continuing concentration of agricultural population in the lowest stratum of the agrarian hierarchy (For details see Chapter I). The extent of state intervention was meagre and the schemes and policies of land reform were mostly used as mechanisms of social control by few.

While the economic condition of the poor peasantry was deteriorating, the political happenings of West Bengal took a new turn. In 1964 there was a split in the Communist Party of India (CPI) leading to the formation of the Communist Party of India (Marxist) (CPI(M)) by the breakaway group. In February 1967 the fourth general election brought the 20 years of unbroken rule by the Congress Party to an end, and an alliance of 14 political parties came to power with the two Communist parties—CPI and CPI(M)— as its constituents.

In late May 1967 the vehement peasant struggle and armed uprising in the Naxalbari Thana of Darjeeling district marked the emergence of a new era in peasant movement in West Bengal, The "Naxalbari Movement" initially was launched under the Darjeeling District Committee of the CPI(M) under the broad Marxist-Leninist-Maoist ideological framework and opted for mass struggle and seizure of power by the guerrilla warfare. The uprising underwent a long-drawn-out struggle between the force organised by the Naxalites and the Zamindar-police combine. The Naxalite leadership provided a forum to form the All-India Coordination Committee of Communist Revolutionaries in November 1967, and later in mid-1969 the Communist Party of India (Marxist-Leninist) (CPI(M-L)) (Ray 1988: 82-83). The Naxalbari movement and the formation of (CPI(M-L)) marked a break in the CPI(M). The movement spread across the country, with Gopiballavpur and Debra Thana of Midnapur, West Bengal, becoming important strongholds of the Naxalites in the late 1960s.

Naxalite Uprising in Gopiballavpur and Debra (1969-71). In 1969, coinciding with the formation of the second United Front Ministry, radical students who were influenced by the Naxalite ideology and led by Ashim Chatterjee and Santosh Rana, organised the poor peasantry of Gopiballavpur and Debra for an armed struggle against the local big landowners and money-lenders. Rana, who had studied at the Presidency College and had been teaching in a high school at Gopiballavpur, hailed from Pitano, a remote village of this Block. The Mallakhatriya caste to which he belonged has a history of rebellion against the rulers.

The Gopiballavpur and Debra Blocks bordered the states of Orissa and Bihar. Both had an overwhelming concentration of poor tribal peasants, many of them were brought from the hill terrain by the landlords. The river Subarna Rekha formed a natural barrier between Gopiballavpur and the rest of the district of Midnapur.

Though the movement was formally launched in Gopiballavpur in August 1969 following the line of "annihilation" of class enemies propagated by Charu Mazumdar, under the auspices of the Bengal-Bihar-Orissa Border Committee (BBOBC) of CPI(ML), at the village level mobilisation of the peasantry had begun much earlier. Initially, the leadership of the movement came from outside and especially from the students of Presidency College, Calcutta. The local leadership emerged gradually as the movement progressed.

Agrarian Social Structure of Shalgeriya on the Eve of the Naxalite Movement: 1969-71. Village Shalgeriya, surrounded by dense forest, was totally isolated from urban influence with not even a dirt road to the nearest town. Most of the village land was unfit for cultivation, being dry and rocky. In the small fertile tract of land of the village traditional variety of paddy was grown using age-old methods. Santal and Bhumij tribes formed the vast majority of the population. There were also a few Thantari (Scheduled Caste) households. The Patnaik caste (Kshatriya) people in the village were descendants of the ex-Naib (popularly known as the Zamindar) of the village. They had controlled the village land since the early 1920s, and held on to their monopoly even in the late 1960s, employing either sharecroppers or agricultural labourers to cultivate it. They clung on to a vast tract of surplus vested land illegally.

The medium, small and marginal cultivators, who belonged to the Scheduled Castes and Scheduled Tribes, occupied the unfertile, barren and dry land. Fifty-two per cent of the village households were of agricultural labourers and 18 per cent of the total households belonged to the category of sharecroppers. The village being very small with single big landowner, the agricultural labourers needed to look for work in other villages including sharecropping.

Table 4.2: Agrarian Classes and Castes in Shalgeriya on the Eve of the Naxalite Movement

Agrarian Class	Caste/ Ethnic Group	Percentage of Households
Very Big Landowners (More than 50 acres)	Upper castes	less than 1%
Medium and Small Category Landowners (2.5 to 10 acres)	Santal, Bhumij	12%
Marginal Landowners (Less than 2.50 acres)	Santal, Bhumij	17%
Sharecroppers	Santal, Bhumij	18%
Landless Agricultural Labourers	Thantari, Santal, Bhumij	52%

Source: Data supplied by the villagers and from old land records of the village.

The village being agriculturally backward, the agricultural labourers were underpaid and remained unemployed during a large part of the year. The landowners employed and terminated the sharecroppers as they wished. They gave loans to the poor peasants at a high rate of interest varying between 100 and 150 per cent per annum. One is reminded of Hamilton's description in 1828 of the Santals of Midnapur:

> Notwithstanding they had their lands on such an easy terms and... their verbal tenures violated, they were said to be naked, half-starved and apparently in the lowest stage of human misery.... These miscreants the Santals, who have but a slender knowledge of the value of money, pay interest at the rate of 100 per cent for their food and nearly 150 per cent for their seeds; so that when their crops are ready little or nothing remains for themselves (Hamilton 1828: 229).

While Shalgeriya's big landowners and those of the neighbouring villages consolidated their stranglehold on the villlage through usury, malafide land transfer, unbridled eviction of sharecroppers and unscrupulous possession over *Benami* lands and near total control over the local market and politico-administrative forces, the wretchedness of the poor peasantry increased. Most of the sharecroppers had been evicted by the landowners. With little access to forestry for the poor, and in the absence of significant development of alternative avenues of economic activities, unemployment and underemployment increased, making the poor peasants more indebted. Whenever any voice was raised against the injustice of the system, landowners effectively crushed the aspiration of the unorganised peasantry with the help of the local administrative authority and the police force. The worst affected were working-class women. Belonging either to the Scheduled Castes or Scheduled Tribes, they were subjected to the age-old patterns of ill treatment and exploitation by the landowners. Starvation, insecurity, ill health, poverty, ignorance and disease dogged every day of their lives.

In the early 1960s the Praja Socialist Party (PSP) started organising the Scheduled Caste and Tribal peasantry against the misuse of forest resources, corruption of forest contractors and government officials and for the distribution of surplus vested lands. But processions and public meetings became the expression of this mobilisation, achieving little result. After its split from the Communist Party of India in 1964 the CPI (M) led Kisan Sabha workers tried to organise a movement against illegal possession of surplus vested land by the big landowners and control of a vast area of land as Devottar (dedicated to God) property by the Devgoswami family of Gopiballavpur. The peasant women became an important force in the process of mobilisation.

Penetration of Naxalite Movement at Shalgeriya. The formation of the United Front Ministry in 1967 gave a fresh impetus to the hitherto dormant popular expectations among the sharecroppers, poor peasants and agricultural labourers of the village. The local Leftist leaders mobilised the poor peasantry to forcibly occupy the surplus vested land which the big landowners illegally clung on to. In this mass mobilisation the women came out of their houses to claim their rights openly.

When this mobilisation was going on under the leadership of the CPI(M) leaders the message of the Naxalbari Movement started penetrating these villages. Santosh Rana, a research student in the Presidency College, took the lead for spreading the revolutionary message in these areas. Subsequently, he accepted a teaching job in a high school (Nayabasan) in Gopiballavpur and started mobilising the peasantry more systematically and for more concrete actions.

When the first left Front Ministry collapsed and President's rule imposed in West Bengal, the big landlords recaptured the occupied lands, terminated the sharecropping contracts and filed fictitious criminal cases against the poor peasantry. The revolutionary movement came on the ascendant once again in 1969 when the second United Front Government came into power. The CPI(M) leaders directed the peasantry to reoccupy the *Benami* and surplus vested lands, to stop the eviction of sharecroppers and to reinstall evicted sharecroppers on their land.

In one case the landowner had cut the standing green paddy from the field that had been cultivated by the sharecroppers; he was trying to prove in the eyes of the law that nothing was cultivated on those plots and that they were in his possession. The agitated peasantry, headed by Santosh Rana, took out a protest procession against the "evil combine" of the landowners and local administration. They demanded from the local police station immediate arrest of the landowner and a suitable compensation to the affected sharecroppers. Most of the peasant women of Shalgeriya spontaneously joined this protest procession. But the big landowners had their way, using police help. Mr. Himansu Kar, a Naxalite leader of that time, reported that when the District Committee of CPI(M) (Midnapur) showed a somewhat casual attitude in the matter, the local leaders of Shalgeriya, approached the CPI(M) State Committee, which, too, did not show much concern. Thus left high and dry, the local leaders decided to localise the movement. They activised their programme to mobilise and unite the sharecroppers, poor peasants and agricultural labourers of the area. In the process, the women became a powerful force for the movement.

The poor peasantry, led by Santosh Rana, started identifying and taking forcible possession of surplus vested land of the landowners both in and outside the village, the women cutting the standing paddy. "Inquilab Zindabad", "Benamia Jamin Dakhal Karo" (Occupy vested land), "Bhagchasi uchched bando karo" (Stop the eviction of the sharecropper), "CPI(M) Zindabad" were the commonly heard slogans of those days. The District Committee of CPI(M), however, observed these actions with mistrust. When the difference between the local and district leaderships widened, the block and village-level leaders of Gopiballavpur headed by Himansu Kar and Santosh Rana started following the Naxalite line of action. The formation of the Coordination Committee of Presidency Group of Naxalites under the leadership of Ashim Chatterjee and Santosh Rana, left no doubt about the local leaders' line of action.

The Naxalite Line of Action. Forty students—about an equal number of boys and girls— came to the Gopiballavpur Block leaving their studies at Presidency College, Calcutta, to conscientise the villagers. Living and working with the villagers as equal to them, the students overcame the villagers' initial mistrust of them. They met the peasantry by night and in small groups to educate them politically, to be united against the landowners and to prepare them for a larger goal to be achieved. Initially the women were passive listeners but gradually they became more active, attending the meetings, processions and maintaining the communication network of the secret meetings. The women students established rapport with the rural women trying to understand their problems.

Within a few weeks of the formation of the Coordination Committee, the Naxalite leaders started to organise public meetings infusing in them the radical message of the Naxalbari Movement. They advised the sharecroppers not to give up the ownership rights of the land they cultivated and the wage labourers to claim higher wages, to claim equal wage for male and female labourers. The newly conscientised poor peasantry were urged to stop repaying the loan to the money-lenders and to occupy the surplus vested lands which were in the illegal possession of the big landowners.

The sleeping village woke up to organised action by the poor peasantry. The tribal peasantry beat drums every night symbolising their victory over the big landowners, and carried their traditional bows and arrows. The women even crossed the boundary of the village to seize the land, crops, ponds and other assets of the landowners.

The Naxalite activities affected law and order in the area. CPI(M) leader Jyoti Basu who later became the Chief Minister, was then in charge of the police portfolio of the second United Front Government. Although some arrests were made and the Eastern Rifles were deployed to help the police in the area, for understandable reasons, the Police Minister was unwilling to do everything to suppress the revolt (Dasgupta 1974:54).

On May 1, 1969 the formation of the Communist Party of India (Marxist-Leninist)—CPI(ML)— was declared in Calcutta by Kanu Sanyal. Henceforth the Naxalite workers of Gopiballavpur began to work under the auspices of the Bengal Bihar Orissa Border Committee of CPI(ML) - BBOBC-CPI(ML). Village committees were also formed in each village. In August 1969 the BBOBC-CPI(ML) accepted the line of the "annihilation of class enemies" propagated by Charu Mazumdar. Promptly, "Red Bases" were established in the forest areas in Gopiballavpur and Debra. Most of the Santal and Bhumij men of Shalgeriya had joined the guerrilla rebels and started taking secret arms training in the forest. They compelled the landowners to surrender their arms to the "Red Guards".

The females of the village initially were not aware of the concept of

Red Guards and their line of action. But as the male activists went underground, they supplied them food in the forest and maintained the communication network for them. Important and urgent messages were always communicated through the women to evade the vigilant eyes of the police. Most women had to spend tense sleepless nights to give or receive messages, to shelter the sick underground activists, and waiting for the male members from the underground to come for food and messages. This was in addition to their running the household economy single-handed.

In September 1969 the Red Guards attacked the house of Ramnarayan Patnaik, the ex-Naib of the village. They blasted country-made bombs and set fire to the house. The landowner, his brother and sons were severely injured. The Red Guards killed a few influential landowners of the neighbouring villages and made attempts on the lives of many landowners and government officials whom they called "class enemies". There was widespread panic and horror among the landed gentry.

The women, however, were not directly involved in the "annihilation programme" though they actively participated in the capturing of lands, seizure of crops, in the demonstrations and processions for the return of the mortgaged property of poor peasants by the money-lenders-cum-landowners, in the struggle for fixation of agricultural wage rate and the time schedule of work. A 52-year-old Santal man of the village, who was the leader of the village committee of the BBOBC-CPI(ML) and was the first person from the village to join the Red Guards to follow the annihilation line, explained that the village women were not associated with the annihilation programme for the following reasons:

— It was a secret decision, shared by only a few.
— Women members were not aware about the happenings of the outside world.
— Women, being soft-hearted by nature, might have felt uneasy with this type of action.

The women, however, helped the Red Guards by informing them about the location and movement of the police. Facing rain, darkness, insecurity and risk to life they supplied them with food and carried their messages.

The annihilation programme continued for years in the Gopiballavpur area. Many landlords were killed, and their guns seized. In the harvesting season their crops were confiscated and distributed among the peasants. The big landlords fled the village, while the small landlords accepted the conditions laid down by the Peasant Committees of the Naxalites. The wages of the agricultural labourers were fixed, and the debts of the peasants to money-lenders were cancelled (Sen 1982: 220). The Naxalites declared the strongholds of their activities as "liberated areas". Shalgeriya along with other villages in the forest was declared a "liberated area". The women of the village were prepared to throw stones, hot water and dust and also to use the bow and the arrow, axes and other available traditional weapons to protect themselves from the police. Along with the men they took all possible measures to prevent the police and other government officials from entering the village. When the males took shelter in the forest to evade arrest, the women organised themselves to prevent police attack on them.

In March 1970 the United Front government collapsed and the Governor took over the reins of administration. Soon thereafter, the police force entered the "liberated areas" in large numbers and crushed the revolt within a short period (Dasgupta 1974: 54). Most of the adult males of the village were arrested. Those who took shelter in the forest and slipped into Bihar and Orissa ultimately surrendered or were arrested. Flogging in public by the police became common in the village. In the absence of the male members of the family and proper direction and leadership, uncertainty and hopelessness descended on the villagers.

Srimatta Nagenbala Rana, mother of Santosh Rana, living in Pitano, a neighbouring village of Shalgeriya recalls those days in the following words:

> While the police action started and most of the male members of the villages were arrested, the women were taking the initiative to protect the family. They were spending sleepless nights with hot water, chilli powder, axe, hoe and with bow and arrow to prevent any sudden attack by the police. The Santal women of Shalgeriya were our bright hope of resistance in those days. While their husbands went to jail the women of Shalgeriya started rebuilding their broken huts, cultivated the small plot of land for years and went out of the village to earn wages to feed the dependants. They accepted all these burdens with a smiling face with the hope of success in the near future. They did not sell out and surrendered their self-respect to any threat. When the husbands came back to the village after imprisonment (may be a short term of six months or a long term of seven years) the women welcomed them with their glittering tears and agony of hearts.

Peasant Movements, Changing Social Relationships and the Peasant Women

The Tebhaga (1946-47) and the Naxalite Movement (1967-71) took place at two different phases of the socio-economic and political formation of the agrarian society of West Bengal. The Tebhaga Movement took place on the eve of the withdrawal of colonial power from India when the poor peasants, tenants and sharecroppers were subjected to the unscrupulous exploitation of the intermediary landowners. The Naxalite Movement took place at another crucial stage of the agrarian and political transformation of the state. This vehement outburst of the discontent of the peasantry was manifested at the juncture of a break in the 20 long years'of Congress rule and the formation of the Leftist-dominated Ministry at the state level. In both movements there was radical political mobilisation of the peasantry. Both movements incorporated, throughout their progression, an organised as well as spontaneous working women's participation. A fallout of this participation was sharp changes in their relationships (see Chart 4.1).

The changing social relationships of working women were characterised by integrity, cohesion and strong unity among 'them' and inimical and hostile relationships against the 'others'. They were the natural allies of the agricultural working class with whom they were tied up with the family, kinship, caste/community, etc. primordial nexus. During the struggle against the landowners-cum-money-lenders and the police/administrative apparatus-combine they manifested strong unity among themselves. The basis of occupational unity thus superseded the primordial ones. The political workers were instrumental in organising and mobilising them against oppression and exploitation and in conscientising them to fight for an egalitarian society. The working women were receptive to their ideologies. In this process the unity of female agricultural workers within their own occupational group was strengthened while their relationships with other groups changed. With the villagers, their relationship disintegrated. While fighting for their own cause they defied the values and norms of the village which subjugated them. The form and extent of the change in their social relationships were greatly influenced by the ideology and the process of mobilisation of the movements under reference.

Chart 4.1: Changing Relationships of Women Agricultural Workers of Khanpur and Shalgeriya in the Pre-Peasant Movement and Peasant Movement Period

Major Social Groups	Pattern of Relationships	
	Pre-Peasant Movement Period	Peasant Movement Period
1. Primordial Groups:		
a. Family Members	Integrated	Integrated Dedicative
b. Kinsmen/ Kinswomen	Cohesive and dutiful	Strongly cohesive
c. Caste/Tribal Members	Cohesive	Strongly cohesive
d. Villagers	Cooperative	Disintegrated
2. Occupational Groups		
a. Female Agricultural Labourers	Friendly	Strongly United
b. Agricultural Labourers Group as a Class	Friendly	Strongly United
c. Landowners-cum-Traditional Money-lenders	Dependent	Inimical
3. Government Machinery		
a. Police/ Administration	—	Hostile/Antagonistic
4. Professional Groups		
a. Political Workers	—	Receptive

The most crucial feature of the change in their social relationship was the commonality in their objectives and actions. The prominent common features of their social relationship in both these peasant movements can be summarised as follows:

(a) All of them experienced a uniform pattern of hostile and inimical social relationships with the landowner-cum-money-lenders.

(b) Their changing social relationships were translated into strong unity among themselves and hostile actions against the landowners-cum-money-lenders and the police administrative apparatus.

(c) In the course of the movement, the females were placed in a situation where they felt they had equal status with their male counterparts.

(d) Their response to this changing social relationship in terms of collective actions against the landowners, etc, was spontaneous and total.

(e) They fought intensively even though the women's issues were not articulated in the broad perspectives of these movements. However, they could find a meaning of their actions within the broad processes of mobilisation.

(f) They opted for uninstitutionalised and radical forms of social actions and collective mobilisation.

V

RURAL WOMEN IN CONTEMPORARY SOCIO-POLITICAL FORMATIONS

This chapter describes the form and extent of women's participation in contemporary peasant movements in West Bengal. The agrarian society of West Bengal has been witness to intense political mobilisation of the peasantry for organised collective actions for significant socio-economic changes since the early 1970s. The important vehicles of these emerging social processes have been the organised and strategic mass mobilisations under the leadership of the leftist political parties for rigorous implementation of land reform laws, activisation of the Village Panchayat for the revitalisation of rural development strategies and launching of various programmes especially for the uplift of the lowest section of society. All these indeed furthered the processes of political mobilisation and politicisation of the rural people affecting pre-existing agrarian relations. Organised peasant movements have been launched in all parts of the state against the feudal tyranny of landowners, and for rapid implementation of land reforms, and labour welfare laws.

In recent years, rural women's response to contemporary peasant movements has been marked by distinctive changes both in content and direction. To be able to understand its major facets the whole gamut of the agrarian social structure of the villages under study are described in this chapter. The emerging socio-economic processes, and the form and direction of women's response to political mobilisation have also been examined here, in the context of both micro and macro socio-political formation of society and state. The chapter is presented in three sections.

In Section I will be presented the broad economic formations and the processes of contemporary political mobilisations of Khanpur and Shalgeriya which experienced vehement Tebhaga and Naxalite Movements in the late 1940s and the late 1960s respectively. In Section-II will be presented another two villages—Panpara (an agriculturally developed village of South Bengal) and Gofanagar (a backward village of North Bengal)— which have no background of any vehement peasant movement. These two sets of villages will provide the background to develop a framework of comparative analysis. In Section III we shall present the emerging trends of commonalities and differences in the broad socio-economic formations of the villages under reference, in the patterns of women's response to collective mobilisation and the variations and similarities in their social relationships across the regions and the state.

SECTION I

VILLAGES WITH BACKGORUND OF EXTENSIVE PEASANT MOVEMENT

Khanpur

Contemporary Khanpur is a rapidly developing village, with high occupational diversification and considerable agricultural modernisation. Though sophisticated farm mechanisation has been meagre, the villagers have introduced large scale cultivation of HYV paddy, jute, oil seeds, etc. and commercialisation of agricultural produce with the intensive use of bio-technological inputs like chemical fertilisers, pesticides, HYV seeds, etc. Around 40 per cent of the cultivable land receives assured supply of water from the deep tube-well of the Irrigation Department of the Government of West Bengal. Many big and medium category landowners have also installed shallow tube-wells with loans from the Rural Development Banks.

The opening up of regular communication networks with the district headquarters, Balurghat and other marketing centres with the construction of a metalled road and introduction of regular bus service since the early 1970s has accelerated economic development. Small Scale business of various sorts has emerged. Large-scale in-migration of East Pakistani (now Bangladesh) Hindu population in the post-independence period, however, has led to phenomenal pressure of population on agriculture on the one hand, and, side by side, a tendency among the villagers to opt for non-agricultural activity as a subsidiary source of income.

Agrarian Social Structure. The agrarian scene of Khanpur has gone through multiple waves of changes in recent years. The main vehicles of this change have been strict imposition of ceiling on landholding, distribution of surplus vested land and rigorous implementation of "Operation Barga"*. Table 5.1 shows that only 22 per cent households of this village are landless. Significantly, of the 289 landowning households 94 have received surplus vested land. Fifty households cultivate land under the sharecropping system; all of them have been brought under Operation Barga.

The upper and middle castes are, however, still at the top of the agrarian hierarchy. While together they represent less than 25 per cent of the households, they control around 48 per cent of the cultivable land. There are only a few landless households among them. The Scheduled Castes, on the other hand, representing more than 52.3 per cent of the village households, account for 75 per cent of the landless households. The Scheduled Castes, Scheduled Tribes, ex-tribes and the Muslim are at the bottom of the agrarian hierarchy. These castes/ethnic groups, while together representing more than 75 per cent of the households, control only about 52 per cent of the cultivable land. Many of them possess land under the sharecropping system, and have received surplus vested land in recent years.

Table 5.1: Landholding by Caste in Khanpur (in acre)

Caste/ Ethnic Group	Percentage of Population	Households					Landholdings (in acres)	
		Total	Landless	Landowning	Sharecropper	Received Surplus Vested Land	Total	Average Size by Household
Upper Castes	5.3	21 (5.7)*	2	19	2	—	127.36 (17.90)†	6.70

* Operation Barga is an institutional measure initiated by the Left Front Government of West Bengal since 1977 with a view to (a) recording the names of the sharecroppers in official records; (b) providing them tenurial security and 75 per cent of the produced crops if inputs of production are supplied by the sharecroppers; and (c) providing them institutional facilities in terms of loans etc.

Middle Castes	19.6	70 (18.9)	5	65	3	1	211.07 (29.66)	3.25
Ex-tribes	18.7	60 (16.2)	5	55	31	11	96.58 (13.57)	1.75
Scheduled Castes	50.3	194 (52.3)	62	132	9	76	245.43 (34.49)	1.86
Scheduled Tribes	3.2	14 (3.8)	3	11	3	6	15.53 (2.18)	1.41
Muslim	2.9	12 (3.2)	5	7	2	—	15.62 (2.19)	2.23
Total	100.0	371 (100)	82 (22.0)	289 (78.0)	50	94	711.59 (99.99)	2.46

Note : * Figures in parentheses in this column are the percentage by caste to the total households.
† Figures in parenthesis in this column are the percentage by caste to the total landholding of the village.

Source: Intensive field survey by the author in 1985-86.

Table 5.2 shows that the agricultural labour households in this village are drawn exclusively from the Scheduled Castes, Scheduled Tribes, Ex-tribes and Muslims. Landless labour households constitute 19.14 per cent of the total households. The landholdings of the Scheduled Castes, Scheduled Tribes, Ex-tribes and Muslim households are centred around the marginal and small categories. Some Ex-tribe and Scheduled Caste households also come in the category of big landowners, but the size of their holding is far below that of the upper and middle caste households. Again, the latter have been the pioneers in introducing modern technology in agriculture. Indeed, the patterns of inequality in landownership have been furthered by the use of modern technique of cultivation by a section of upper caste-cum-class households in recent years. Small and marginal cultivators altogether represent around 68 per cent of the households and control only around 43 per cent of the land; the medium and big cultivators, while representing less than 10 per cent of the households, control more than 57 per cent of the land.

Table 5.2: Size of Landholding by Caste in Khanpur

Agrarian Category by Landholding (in acres)	Upper Castes	Middle Castes	Ex-tribes	Scheduled Castes	Scheduled Tribes	Muslims	Total No. of households	Total Land holding
Landless :A (Labourers)	—	—	3	60	3	5	71 (19.14)*	—
Landless:B Business/ Servicemen	2	5	2	2	—	—	11 (2.96)	—
Marginal (0-2.50)	8	35	38	103	9	6	199 (53.64)	128.50 (18.06)
Small (2.50-5.00)	4	21	9	17	2	-	53 (14.29)	175.53 (24.67)
Medium (5.00-10.00)	3	5	6	9	—	1	24 (6.47)	169.63 (23.84)
Big (10.00+)	4	4	2	3	—	—	13 (3.50)	237.93 (33.44)
Total	21	70	60	194	14	12	371 (100.00)	711.59 (100.00)

Notes: * Figures in parenthesis in this column refer to percentage of number of households.
† Figures in parenthesis in this column refer to percentage of total landholding.

Source : Intensive field survey by the author in 1985-86.

Women's Work Participation. The agrarian class position and the traditional caste and ethnic values have a composite bearing on the nature and form of women's work participation. While the working-class women are predominantly from the Scheduled Castes, Scheduled Tribes and Ex-tribal groups, in recent years, women of the upper and middle castes have joined white-collar jobs.

Statistically, the rate of women's work participation has been moderate, with only 37 per cent of the total number in the work force (Table 5.3). It should still be noted that 40 per cent of the working women are in the non-agricultural sector which comprises service, business and household industry and household service as maid-servants.

No Muslim woman is in the work force. Among the upper and the middle castes work participation is marginal, being 6.8 and 2.8 per cent respectively. The traditional values of the upper and middle castes and of the Muslims are against women's extra-mural manual activities. Thus, women of these caste and ethnic groups while constituting around 28 per cent of the female population contribute only 2.4 per cent of the female work force.

Women's work participation rates among the ex-tribes and the Scheduled Tribes are 65 and 72 per cent respectively. While representing only 22 per cent of the female population, they together contribute more than 42 per cent of the female work force. Also, differences between male and female work participation rates among them are insignificant. Of the total women workers of the ex-tribes 26 per cent are in the business and households industry, 9 per cent work as cultivators and 65 per cent as agricultural labourers. Occupational diversification is thus high among them. The Scheduled Tribe women on the other hand are exclusively agricultural labourers, signifying their low economic status and absence of occupational diversification among them.

The Scheduled Caste women while representing 50.5 per cent of the female population, constitute 58.6 per cent of the female work force of the village. Some important features of their work participation are noted below:

(a) The Scheduled Castes are not a homogeneous category.
(b) The caste values of the Rajbansi and Polia generally work against women's participation in extra-mural agricultural activities.
(c) Sanskritisation has been accompanied by withdrawal of women (especially in households with substantial landholding) from extra-mural manual activities.
(d) The Colkamar and Mali women work as agricultural labourers and construction workers mainly, while the Rajbansi and Polia women are taking advantage of new avenues of economic activities.
(e) In recent years because of economic complusion Mali women have resorted to agricultural wage earning.
(f) Of the total female work force among the Schedules Castes around 50 per cent is in the non-agricultural sector.

Table 5.3: Work Participation by Caste and Sex in Khanpur

Caste/ Ethnic Group	Total Population		Cultivation		Agricultural Labourers		Public Service		Business and Household Industry		Household Service as Maid-servants	Total No. of Workers		Percentage to Total Female Workers
	M	F	M	F	M	F	M	F	M	F	F	M	F	F
Upper Castes	45	44 (5.5)*	20	—	1	—	2	3	6	—	—	23 (64.4)†	3 (6.8)†	1.0
Middle Castes	178	150 (18.9)	71	—	13	—	6	4	12	—	—	102 (57.3)	4 (2.6)	1.4
Ex-tribes	164	149 (18.7)	17	10	55	62	—	—	32	25	—	104 (63.4)	97 (65.0)	32.9
Scheduled Castes	438	402 (50.5)	38	24	212	63	—	—	21	63	23	271 (61.8)	173 (43.0)	58.6
Scheduled Tribes	29	25 (3.1)	—	—	21	18	—	—	—	—	—	21 (72.4)	18 (72.0)	6.1
Muslims	22	26 (3.3)	6	—	10	—	—	—	—	—	—	16 (—)	— (—)	.0
Total	876	796 (100)	152	34 (11.5)@	312	143 (48.4)@	8	7 (2.3)@	71	88 (30.0)@	23 (7.8)@	543 (61.9)	295 (37.0)	100.00

Notes: * The figures in parenthesis in this column are the percentages of the women population by caste to the total number of women of the village.
† The figures in parenthesis in these columns are the male and female work participation rates, i.e. percentages of workers to the male or female population respectively.
@ The figures in the parentheses are the percentages of women workers by the major category to the total women workers of 295.

Source: Intensive field survey by the author in 1985-86.

A break-up of the women's work participation by industrial categories shows that 48.4 per cent and 11.5 per cent of them respectively belong to the category of agricultural labourers and cultivators; 30 per cent are in business and household industry, 2.3 per cent in public service and 7.8 per cent in household service as maid-servants. The tendency to shift to non-agricultural economic activities has been furthered by the process of sanskritisation.

Forms of Work Contract in Agriculture. Female agricultural labourers may be Betisoul Khetmajur (casual labour) or Betisoul Chuktidars (contract labour). The Betisoul Khetmajur enter into temporary (mostly day-to-day) contract with the employers. Their wage varies from season to season. They are paid both in cash and in kind and usually get Rs. 1.50 to Rs. 2.50 plus 3 sers (1 ser = 700 grams) of paddy as their daily wage. In monetary terms they get an average of Rs. 5 per day. They are to work from 7 (or 7.30) a.m. to 5 (or 5.30) p.m. with a break for lunch for about one and a half hours. A female agricultural labourer usually gets around 235 days of employment in a year.

The above is a free casual labourer. There is also casual labour of semi-attached nature. Called *Dadani*—because this relationship is based on a loan termed as *Dadan*—they work on the basis of a "beck-and-call" relationship. Under *Dadan*, female agricultural workers take loan of Rs. 20 to Rs. 60 from the landowner in the lean season. Thereby they oblige themselves to work in his field in the peak season but are free to work elsewhere if he does not need their service. The *Dadan* workers get a fixed Re. 1 (which is deducted against the loan) plus 3 sers of paddy as daily wage while for the free female laburers the wage rate usually goes up to Rs. 2.50 plus 3.5 sers of paddy. In May-June 1986, 65 female agricultural labourers took Dadan loan.

Betisoul Chuktidar — contract labour— is the more popular system of female wage labour. A contract is taken for transplanting paddy, weeding in jute or Aush paddy (pre-monsoon paddy) lands and harvesting of paddy. Often, the entire household becomes a working unit. Among the Mahatos (ex-tribes) there are a few big joint families with more than 20 members and they prefer to work under the contract system. It gives an opportunity to the female labourers for more earnings and also benefits the landowner because of its element of free enterprise.

In the case of female agricultural labourers, bargaining capacity is uneven. This is because their economic position varies based on sharecropping system, small and marginal sizes of landholdings, debt obligations, access to alternative sources of earnings and forms of work contract.

Under the sharecropping system of cultivation, the female labourers as members of the sharecropper's household maintain an extra-economic relation with the landowner. They are to work in his field in the peak season for a stipulated wage which is usually lower than the market rate. *Operation Barga* has considerably reduced the anomalies of this system, but the system itself is still prevalent.

The majority of female agricultural labourers belong to households of marginal cultivators. Fifty-six per cent of these households possess land below one acre size, 21 per cent between 1.00 and 2.50 acres and the rest 23 per cent households possess 2.50 acres and above size of land. Only 40 per cent of these households have agricultural implements and draught animals. To cultivate their tiny plot of land the rest borrow inputs like the plough and the cattle from the big landowners, who supply these either free of cost or at low cost to their "reliable" farm servants. The result is a lowered bargaining capacity for the latter.

Indebtedness is another limitation on bargaining capacity. Around 23 per cent of these labour households are indebted to the landowners. Female labourers with alternative economic activities and from households with relatively higher landholding, and women workers who work under contract have on the other hand, a higher bargaining capacity.

Alternative Economic Activities. Paddy husking and making of Muri (puffed rice) and Chira (flattened rice) are important avenues of self-employment and alternative economic activities at Khanpur. Though 30 per cent of the female work force are engaged in these business activities primarily, for a large number of others they provide a subsidiary source of income especially during the lean agricultural season.

These activities have expanded considerably in recent years. The village has also been well connected with the marketing centres. The Rural Development Bank has sanctioned loans to 77 households for these small businesses. A female worker earns between Rs. 30 to Rs. 40 per week throughout the year from these businesses.

The benefits of most of these progressive developments are, however, limited mainly to Mahato (ex-tribes) and Rajbansi and Polia (Scheduled Castes) women, bringing about sharp diversities between them on the one hand, and the Mali, Colkamar (Scheduled Castes) and Santal (Scheduled Tribe) women on the other. Change has touched the latter but marginally. Ethnic background, levels of literarcy, and exposure to the outside world have played crucial roles in the women's receptivity to alternative allied-agricultural economic activities. The Mali women have joined agricultural wage earning only recently. Earlier, they had been working primarily as domestic servants. The Mahato women have keenly taken to business very recently; outdoor agricultural farm operation and agricultural wage earning also have equal importance for them. For the Colkamar women agricultural wage work has got the highest priority; households farm operations and recently introduced business activities come only next to it. For the Santal women outdoor household farm operation is very pronounced and agricultural wage earning is the principal activity.

In the light of the above, the following sub-groups of female work force in Khanpur emerge:

(a) Agricultural labourers:
  (i) Free casual labourers;
  (ii) *Dadani*;
(b) Cultivators-cum-agricultural labourers;
(c) Business women;
(d) Agricultural labourers-cum-business women;
(e) Agricultural labourers-cum-cultivators-cum-business women;
(f) Business women-cum-cultivators;
(g) Service women.

As will be seen later, though these sub-categories are not exclusive in nature, they are of vital sociological importance, for the position a female worker holds determines her agrarian social relation to a large extent. These sub-categories have both socio-economic and political implications. The form and extent of women's participation in the process of collective political mobilisation have been significantly shaped by the pattern of the emergence of various sub-categories among them.

Political Mobilisation and Women's Response. The patterns of political mobilisation in Khanpur have undergone substantial changes since the United Left Front (ULF) Government came in to power in West Bengal in 1977. Mass mobilisation had been initiated in an earlier phase between 1967 and 1969 when the United Front (UF) came to power for the first time, but these were not sustained for long. During this phase, the formation of the Leftist-dominated government aroused considerable expectations among the lower section of the agrarian society. Their leaders led the movement for occupying the surplus vested land, cutting the standing paddy and seizure of crops from the granaries of the big landowners, and elicited popular participation. But this movement was sporadic and it collapsed with the fall of the United Front government.

It needs to be noted, however, that this was the first mobilisation, in post-independence India, of peasants for collective action against the local landlords. The political mobilisation in Khanpur was not isolated; rather it was part of the tactical mobilisation of the peasantry which was taking place all over the state under the leadership of the Communist parties. Women's participation in this mobilisation, however, was marginal even though the Communist party workers tried to rekindle in them memories of the Tebhaga Movement. In the days of the Tebhaga Movement, the Rajbansi women had been in the forefront; they were now virtually silent. So were the Polia and Mahato women. It was the Santal and Colkamar women who now came to the fore.

Politicisation and political mobilisation in recent years have been closely interlinked with all aspects of the villagers' lives. The activities initiated by the United Left Front (ULF) government of West Bengal since 1977 have catalysed them. Political party workers of the Communist Party of India (Marxist) (CPI (M)), Communist Party of India (CPI) and the Revolutionary Socialist Party (RSP) have been mobilising the poor peasantry of Khanpur for the distribution of surplus vested land, implementation of *Operation Barga*, for institutional credits to the small and marginal peasants and for the small businessmen, for pension to the fighters of the Tebhaga movement, old peasants and to the widows and also for pressurising government officials to initiate measures like food for work, and other relief. Gherao, strike, procession, meeting, demonstrations etc. have been the major forms of collective political action for mobilisation. The institution of Gram Panchayat is often used to implement the major decisions taken at the wider level of society and also to focus the local issues at the wider level.

Women's participation in political mobilisation has been segmental and sporadic—and what has been there of it has been seldom subject to the factionalism of the party workers of CPI(M), CPI, and RSP. Significantly, while working women take part in agitation and political mobilisation non-workers and housewives stay away. The economic position and occupational pattern of the female workers thus play a crucial role in shaping the nature and extent of their participation in political activities.

Recently, the working conditions of female agricultural workers have received wide attention. The local leaders of the Leftist parties have sought to mobilise female agricultural labourers against the big landowners on issues pertaining to unequal wages between male and female, unregulated hours of work, low wages, uneven wage structure, seasonal variations in the wage structure, humiliation of the labourers by the landowners, and so on.

In Khanpur women's participation in agricultural workers' strike has been an important aspect of the political process, but the nature and extent of their participation have not been uniform. The women's participation is valued by the political workers for three reasons specific to the local context: (a) female workers' participation would only partially affect the household economy; (b) a sizeable portion of the male labourers of the village are attached as annual permanent farm servants, while the females are mainly casual labourers; and (c) the strikes are organised mainly in the transplantation seasons when the female labourers are urgently needed in this operation.

The first agricultural labour strike was organised in July 1984. It was the peak transplantation season. The village Pradhan (elected chief of the Gram Panchayat) organised this strike in collaboration with the female wing of the CPI(M) organisation of the village. They undertook a door-to-door campaign of the agricultural labour households for the strike. The latter were organised to stay away from work until the following demands were met: (a) implementation of Minimum Wage Act, i.e. Rs. 14.90 as daily wage to all agricultural labourers; (b) equal wages to male and female; (c) stipulated 8 hours of work in a day; and (d) no wage variation on the basis of peak and lean seasons. A procession was organised on the day before the strike.

On strike day, the males (annual farm servants) initially hesitated to join work, but as the day advanced they joined work and were followed by an important section of the Mahato women who work under the contract system. The weakness of the organisation and the diversity of the agricultural working class were thus exposed within a few hours of the strike. The strike was, however, strongly supported and maintained by most of the Colkamar, Mali and Santal women who were mostly casual labourers. In the evening the landowners, most of whom have joined the Leftist banner in recent years, in an informal talk declared enhancement of the agricultural labourers' wage of all categories by 50 paise. Some political workers wanted to carry on the strike indefinitely for the full implementation of their demands, but the next day, barring a few Santal and the majority of the Colkamar women, most women agricultural labourers joined work. On the third day the strike came to an end when the leaders advised the labourers to join work and declared the suspension of the strike temporarily. The women agricultural labourers of Colkamar and a few Santal households had been ready to continue the strike and accused the local leaders and other labourers of being *Chata* (pets) of the landowners.

In July 1985, in the peak transplantation period another strike was organised by the Leftist workers on a directive by the party headquarters. This strike also was marked by spontaneous participation by the Colkamar, and a few Santal and Mali women labourers; and non-spontaneous and sporadic participation of the Mahato and a section of Santal women labourers. The strike ended that evening, again with the rise of the wage of all categories of labourers by another 50 paise for the peak season.

Heterogeneity has emerged among the agricultural work force of Khanpur. The Mahato women have been able to get substantial benefit out of the emerging new avenues of economic opportunities. They also mortgage land from the other groups of female agricultural labourers, mostly Colkamar. They have shown less interest in political conflicts. On the other hand, the Colkamar, and the Mali females who have not been able to get much benefit from the new economic opportunities, and have been engaged in agricultural wage earning mainly, have shown the highest interest in political agitation. While the Santal women who fall in the above category join them, those whose family has land under sharecropping system and whose male members work as permanent farm servants avoid political agitation.

Factionalism worsens the divide. Political mobilisations sponsored by the RSP and CPI are not always backed by CPI(M) workers, and vice versa. The economic interest of the working class has on many occasions been made subordinate to the political interest of different factions.

Shalgeriya

Shalgeriya has remained one of the most backward villages of Midnapur. Though the extent of its poverty and agricultural backwardness were brought into the limelight during the Naxalite Movement in 1967-71, no substantial change has taken place in its economic structure. The organisation of agricultural production is still backward with predominant use of traditional tools and technology and subsistence crop cultivation. A vast area of its dry and rocky land has remained uncultivated. An irrigation canal constructed across the village is dry at its source. Scope for alternative economic activities is also bleak. Free access of the villagers to the forest was put under severe restrictions even though there has been large-scale commercial felling of trees. Agriculture therefore remains the mainstay of livelihood resulting in mounting pressure of population on land. Since agriculture cannot absorb the entire labour force of the village, a significant section of the surplus labour force migrate seasonally to other agriculturally developed districts. Seasonal out-migration has now become an established feature of Shalgeriya's social scene.

Agrarian Social Structure. A few important measures have been initiated in Shalgeriya since the mid-1970s aiming to reduce agrarian inequality and to further economic development. The distribution of surplus vested land, strict implementation of the ceiling restriction on landholding and institutionalising the sharecropping system of cultivation through *Operation Barga* are some of these. Though these have affected the pre-existing agrarian social structure, their results as far as the economic position of the lowest section of society is concerned are hardly spectacular. To give one instance: More than sixty acres of deforested land were taken over from the ex-Naib of the village and distributed among the poor peasants. But the distributed plots are very small, mostly infertile and dry. The villagers are expected to level these plots for cultivation but if they were to do that leaving their paid labour, they would starve. Of the 73 plots, 57 are dry and barren. Only 22 allottees have taken the initiative to bring their plots under cultivation.

Sharecropping is an important feature of Shalgeriya's agrarian social structure. Though the sharecroppers have been brought under the *Operation Barga*, their economic position remains grim.

Table 5.4 shows that there are 95 landowning households in the village. Only 10 possess land under the sharecropping system and 73 have received surplus vested land. Twelve households are without land. The upper castes are at the top of the agrarian hierarchy with all the four upper caste households possessing land measuring an average of 11.5 acres, which is the highest average size of landholding. The upper castes constituting less than 4 per cent of the households, control more than 36 per cent of the land, which includes all the fertile tracts. The Scheduled Castes and Scheduled Tribes on the other hand not only occupy rocky and unfertile land, their average size of landholding is also meagre with 0.44 acre and 1.04 acre respectively. While representing more than 96 per cent of the households, they altogether control only around 64 per cent of the land.

Table 5.4 : Landholding by Caste in Shalgeriya (in acres)

Caste/ Ethnic Group	Percent-age of Popu-lation	Households					Landholdings	
		Total	Land-less	Land-owning	Share-cropper	Received Surplus Vested Land	Total	Average Size by House-hold
Upper Castes	2.73	4 (3.7)*	—	4	—	—	46.00 (36.19)*	11.5
Scheduled Castes	25.04	32 (30.0)	9	23	—	23	10.32 (8.12)	0.44
Scheduled Tribes	72.23	71 (66.3)	3	68	10	50	70.79 (55.69)	1.04
Total	100.00	107 (100)	12	95	10	73	127.11 (100.00)	1.34

Note: * The figures in parentheses in these columns are the percentages by caste to the total household and landholding of the village respectively.

Source: Intensive field survey by the author in 1985-86.

The caste and class hierarchies of the village are intertwined. Table 5.5 shows that the bottom of the agrarian hierarchy—the landless, marginal and small cultivator households—is entirely occupied by the Scheduled Caste and Scheduled Tribe households, while the medium and big cultivators are overwhelmingly represented by upper caste household. Thus, only around 4 per cent of the village households form the middle and upper strata of the caste and agrarian hierarchy while 96 per cent are at the bottom.

The working-class women are completely from the bottom of the caste and class hierarchy. The form and extent of their work participation are widely determined by the economic positions of these households, and by the broad processes of socio-economic formations of the village.

Table 5.5 : Caste and Class in Shalgeriya

Agrarian Categories by Landholding (in acres)	Upper Castes	Scheduled Castes	Scheduled Tribes	No. of Households	Landholding
Landless	—	9	3	12 (11.21)*	—
Marginal (0-2.50)	—	23	59	82 (76.64)	63.11 (49.65)*
Small (2.50-5.00)	—	—	8	8 (7.48)	12.00 (9.44)
Medium (5.00-10.00)	3	—	1	4 (3.74)	36.00 (28.32)
Big (10.00)	1	—	—	1 (0.93)	16.00 (12.59)
Total	4	32	71	107 (100.00)	127.11 (99.99)

Notes : * Figures in parentheses refer to percentage.

Source : Intensive field survey by the author in 1985-86.

Women's Work Participation. Women's work participation is significantly high at 69.6 per cent. No upper caste woman is at extra-mural work. Among the Scheduled Castes women's work participation rate is 77.4 per cent which is the highest in the village, followed by the 69.2 per cent work participation rate for the Scheduled Tribe women. Female work participation rate in these two categories is astonishingly higher than even that of males. This is mostly because while many young boys have joined school, girls have joined the labour market; and while many old males of above 60 years of age have withdrawn from the labour force, a substantial number of women of this age group are still in the labour force.

Of the women workers, 91 per cent are agricultural labourers; only 5 per cent are engaged in cultivation and 4 per cent in business and household industry. In the absence of alternative avenues of economic activity, and because of the predominantly marginal and small size of landholding women's work participation has been highly concentrated in agricultural wage earnings.

Table 5.6: Work Participation by Caste and Sex in Shalgeriya

Caste/ Ethnic Group	Total Population		Cultivation		Agricultural Labourers		Service		Business and Household Industry		Total No. of Workers		Percentage to Total Workers
	M	F	M	F	M	F	M	F	M	F	M	F	F
Upper Castes	8	7 (2.6)*	3	—	—	—	2	—	—	—	5	—	—
Scheduled Castes	67	71 (27.0)	—	—	39	47	—	—	10	8	49 (73.1)†	55 (77.4)†	30.0
Scheduled Tribes	213	185 (70.4)	8	9	116	119	—	—	—	—	124 (58.2)	128 (69.2)	70.0
Total	288	263 (100.00)	11	9 (5.0)@	155	166 (91.0)@	2	—	10	8 (4.0)@	178	183 (69.6)	100.00

Notes: * The figures in parentheses in this column are the percentages of the female population by caste to the total female population of the village.

†The figures in parentheses are in these columns are the percentages of male and female workers to the total male and female population respectively.

@ The figures in parentheses are the percentages of women workers by the major category to the total women workers.

Source: Intensive field survey by the author in 1985-86.

Forms of Work Contract. Contract work on day-to-day basis is the only category of female agricultural labour in the village. Wages are subject to variation. Such workers are called Kamins. The Kamins usually resort to Namal (seasonal migration to other districts) for work. Within the village they are to work from sunrise to sunset with a two-hour break for lunch. They usually get 1.5 to 2 Mann (one Mann is roughly equivalent to 1.5 kilograms) of paddy plus breakfast as their daily wages. Payment is mostly in kind, which in monetary terms amounts to around Rs. 3 per day. A Kamin on an average gets 190 to 201 mandays of work in the village and its environs in one year.

Namal, according to local vocabulary, means spatial movement of people to areas where there are abundant water resources and agricultural activity. In real terms, it implies seasonal migration of the villagers to the agriculturally developed districts for wage earning. The female agricultural labourers migrate twice in a year with other able-bodied members of the family to the agriculturally developed areas of Burdwan and Hooghli districts for work, even 200 kilometres away from home. The landowners contact them through middlemen locally known as *Dalal*.

Migration takes place in three different phases of agricultural operations. The first phase is in mid-Ashar (July-August). The migrant labour work for about two months and return to their village by the middle of Bhadra (September-October) to work there mostly for transplantation of paddy and harvesting of jute. The second phase of migration takes place by the end of Kartik (November-December), and gives them substantial earnings. They migrate just after the *Badhan* ceremony (worship of the bullock) of the tribes: and return home just before the *Pushna* ceremony (the pie ceremony), which takes place on the last day of Poush (January-February). The third phase of migration takes place after the *Pushna* ceremony. This time mainly the males migrate and return after a month. As migrant labourers, they are usually paid Rs. 5 plus the required rice, vegetable, oils, fuels, etc. to prepare three meals in a day. The landowners also arrange temporary shelters for them.

In 1985-86, 78 per cent of the female agricultural labourers of the village migrated there in the transplantation season and 85 per cent in the harvesting season. All female agricultural labourers of the village have had experience of out-migration.

When the villagers migrate, the village wears a deserted look. The females who stay back have to look after the family and property. Those who stay back are the infirm, the old, expecting mothers and those with infants or those with livestock and unfinished household farm activities.

Female migrant labourers save more money than the males since the latter spend more on drink, smoke and other entertainment. The cash income, however, has not made any marked change on the economy of the village. Most labour households still cook food only once a day. Only a few households light a lamp in the night, the use of even a kerosene lamp being a luxury. Starvation, insecurity, ill health are their eternal lot. Namal also has led to a gradual increase of venereal diseases and abortions among the tribal women, undermining both the health and institutional structure of the village society.

In *Namal* contract, the women workers' bargaining power is limited. They, however, do not bargain since (a) the landowners provide them shelter, fuel and utensils, (b) they earn more than in their own village, and (c) they are paid on par with the agricultural labourers of that area. Many male labourers of the village have stayed back permanently in the agriculturally developed areas, having taken loans from their masters. Their women usually work in the field of these masters. In the village also they are subjugated in the following ways:

(a) They are low paid throughout the year irrespective of peak and lean seasons of agricultural operation.
(b) They are paid less than their male counterparts.
(c) There are no fixed hours of work.

Women workers involved in household farm activities alone are virtually absent in this village. Some women primarily work on their own farm and then opt for wage earnings either in the village or they migrate with the male members of the family. There, indeed, have not emerged distinctive diversities among the women agricultural workers of the village based on work participation on the household farm.

Alternative Economic Activities. There is no strong base for alternative economic activities in Shalgeriya. On the contrary, the traditional base from which the women workers could gain considerable economic support has been destroyed because of deforestation. Earlier women could collect sufficient roots, fruits, wood, tubers and wild vegetables from the forest. Much of the forest has now disappeared and whatever remains of it is barred to the villagers.

There are only few old Scheduled Caste women primarily making and marketing brass idols, which is their traditional craft. They barter the idols in the village and in its neighbourhood for old utensils, foodgrains etc. This business, too, is declining because of the high price of raw materials and marketing problems.

Collecting *Sal* leaves, *Dantan* (Sal-sticks used to brush the teeth) and firewood from the forest for sale is another economic activity of the tribal women, but this is only seasonal and not very paying. Some women brew *Choyani*, a traditional country liquor, but this is illegal and not enough rewarding economically.

In the absence of rewarding alternative economic activities, female work participation in Shalgeriya is centred around agriculture alone. Here, they display some important common socio-economic features:

(a) The working class women belong to the poorest section of the caste and class hierarchy.
(b) They experience the same levels of poverty, unemployment, starvation, frustration and illiteracy.
(c) They are pushed to migrate seasonally to other districts for work.
(d) They experience equal form of sexual subjugation and discrimination.
(e) Their lives are extreme drudgery.

Political Mobilisation and Women's Response. The process of political mobilisation in Shalgeriya is at a crucial juncture, and the women have been in its forefront. It is they who have maintained an unbroken link between the vehement Naxalite Movement of 1967-71 and the present phase of political mobilisation.

When the police came down heavily on the Naxalite Movement in the early 1970s, the peasantry were in a disarray. Even when a large number of Naxalite detainees were released in the mid-1970s and political activities resumed, the villagers' discontent had to remain latent under the state of emergency rule and strong police vigilance.

In the elections of 1977 the Congress (I) ministries were trounced both at the Centre and in the State Assembly, catalysing once again the peasant movement. In the State Assembly election a group of Naxalites of this area headed by Santosh Rana following the line of Satya Narayan Sinha, decided to participate in the electoral politics. Though other radical sections of Naxalites sharply criticised this decision, it created a new environment for political participation and brought significant and qualitative change in the process of political mobilisation in this area.

Santosh Rana was in jail when he filed his nomination papers to contest for the State Assembly constituency of Gopiballavpur as the CPI(ML)-supported candidate. For the repressed peasants of Shalgeriya, this news was dynamite. Enthusiasm was at a fever pitch. Memories of sacrifices and glory of the vehement Naxalite movement were still fresh in the villagers' minds. To them, Santosh Rana was a living myth, symbol of organisational unity and sacrifice. With them now once again openly mingled the Naxalites, who had been inhumanly tortured by the police, had been subjected to prolonged and cumbersome trials and incarceration, their families ruined, rousing once again the peasants consciousness. In the days of police repression of Naxalites, the women had fared the worst. Tortured, humiliated and degraded, they had gone through many years of uncertainty. With one voice they now came forward, to campaign for the men who symbolised all their struggle and hopes. Nagenbala Rana, the mother of Santosh Rana, and her colleagues addressed public meetings and canvassed door-to-door, rousing the village women to the awareness of who their "class enemies" were and urging them to "eliminate them from society" by casting their vote in favour of the "friends of the revolution".

Santosh Rana was elected in the 1977 assembly election with a wide margin. This group of Naxalites thereafter began mobilising the rural poor of the area for political action through "institutionalised means". Since 1977, the working-class women of Shalgeriya have been mobilised for the village panchayat, State Assembly and parliamentary elections, for the implementation of various land reform laws, protection of the forest and pressurising the government machinery for initiating various welfare measures for development of their area. Efforts were made to distribute surplus vested land, protect the interest of the sharecroppers, promote work avenues during the lean seasons, and to undertake constructive work.

Santosh Rana was defeated in the State Assembly elections of 1982. But the process of mass mobilisation he introduced continues to operate. Regarding women's participation in this phase of Naxalite Movement he points out that:

> the Naxalites have started an elaborate programme to organise working class women to fight the bourgeois state order. The Naxalites feel that the elevation of the economic status of the toiling masses and the withering away of the bourgeois state order are possible only through uninterrupted struggle. To make the struggle uninterrupted and enduring, women will have to be brought into the struggle. In the Indian context participation in electoral politics and

uninterrupted mass mobilisation against local boureoisie simultaneously are the means to an end. And we are working in this direction only. . . .

In recent years, the complexion of political mobilisation has undergone a change. An important section of the Naxalite leaders at block and district levels have defected to the CPI(M). The village has also been involved in the Jharkhand Mukti Morcha (JMM). There has been triangular political mobilisation for collective action, among the activists and followers of CPI(M), CPI(ML) and JMM. They have mobilised the villagers on local issues such as low wages, sex-based wage discrimination, distribution of surplus vested and forest lands, poor development measures, and so on. All political parties have sought to bring the womenfolk under their own banner. The Naxalites' agenda for women's liberation is for the uninterrupted mobilisation of women against

(a) exploitation of women in society and family and sex based inequality;
(b) Conservatism and ignorance;
(c) inequality in work and education;
(d) wage discrimination;
(e) exhibiting women's body in advertisement, cinema, drama, etc.;
(f) purdah and dowry system;
(g) rape and physical exploitation;
(h) prostitution;
(i) polygamy;
(j) slavery of women.

(Nari Mukti Andoloner Karma Suchi, (Bengali) unpublished document, 1985:3)

Over the years, dross has crept into the process of political mobilisation. Political workers and local leaders have been changing their party allegiances like suits of clothes. The Village Panchayat is bogged down in factionalism. The women have been shifting their support between political parties entirely on considerations of short-term gains for themselves. The ideological differences between the different left political parties do not mean much to them; neither do issues relating to Afghanistan, Kampuchea, Vietnam, Sri Lanka or Angola. The agenda for Women's Liberation Movement does not touch their immediate, deprived lives.

All this notwithstanding, women's political mobilisation for collective action has been spontaneous and continuous process in Shalgeriya. Women workers are frequently organised by one political party or another to organise demonstrations in front of government offices and also to Gherao government officers to undertake specific development measures, to start food for work, relief work, etc. The Naxalites have initiated programmes to make the women aware about their health care and food and education of the children. Processions, meetings and demonstrations have been for higher and equal wages for women. Women's response to organised political action has cut across factionalism, depending on the issues involved.

Women agricultural workers are usually mobilised in the agricultural lean season when jobs are scarce within or outside the village. They are bleak days for the economically strapped families and they can be easily mobilised for collective action that promises them particular economic benefit. Tension, aggressive propaganda and frequent agitations characterise this political mobilisation. Though, because of diverse political persuasions the unity of the agricultural working class has not been forged, their hostility and collective action have been directed against the big landowners and government officials.

SECTION II

VILLAGES WITHOUT BACKGROUND OF EXTENSIVE PEASANT MOVEMENT

Panpara

Panpara is a developed village, agriculturally, economically and socially. There is regular and assured supply of water for irrigation from the Damodar Valley Corporation canal and deep and shallow tube-wells of the Comprehensive Area Development Project of Boinchi. Most of the small, medium and big landowners also have installed privately owned shallow tube-wells. Commercial crops are profitably grown. There is a good network of communication around the village. Potential for alternative economic activities is present in the form of small business of various types.

Agrarian Social Structure. The land in Panpara is very fertile. Assured supply of irrigation water and intensive use of sophisticated agricultural technologies, namely tractors, seed-wheels, weeders, spray machines, threshers, HYV seeds, chemical fertilisers, pesticides and so on, have markedly increased their yield. The cropping pattern also has changed to accommodate the large-scale cultivation of cash crops. These have affected the patterns of ownership, control and use of land and the dynamics of social relations of the village.

The landholding pattern in Panpara is sharply unequal and follows the traditional line of caste and ethnic social groupings. Though the Scheduled Castes and Scheduled Tribes together account for around 40 per cent of the village household, they occupy less than 8 per cent of the village land; 83 per cent of the landless households belong to these social categories. The upper castes, on the other hand, while constituting only 44.6 per cent of the households, occupy around 80 per cent of the cultivable lands; only 5.5 per cent of the landless households belong to this category. The middle castes, representing 15.5 per cent of the households occupy around 13 per cent of the cultivable lands (Table 5.7). The upper and the middle caste groups are comparatively affluent. They have employed most of the modern techniques of cultivation and have improved their income and life style significantly in recent years.

Table 5.7: Landholding by Caste in Panpara (in acres)

Caste/ Ethnic Group	Percentage of Population	Households					Landholding	
		Total	Landless	Landowning	Leased in as Sharecropper	Holders of "Patta"	Total	Average Size by Household
Upper Castes	44.9	66 (5.5)*	3 (67.0)†	63 (67.0)†	4	—	245.17 (79.74)*	3.89
Middle Castes	17.4	23 (14.8)	8 (16.0)	15 (16.0)	1	—	39.53 (12.86)	2.64
Scheduled Castes	20.7	29 (19.6)	26 (48.2)	3 (3.2)	1	—	1.95 (0.63)	0.65
Scheduled Tribes	17.0	30 (20.3)	17 (31.8)	13	13	—	20.80 (6.77)	1.60
Total	100.00	148 (100.0)	54 (100.0)	94	19	—	307.45 (99.99)	3.27

Notes: *The figures in parentheses in these columns are the percentages by caste to the total household and landholding of the village respectively.
† The figures in parentheses in these columns are the percentages to the total landless and landowning households respectively.

Source: Intensive field survey by the author in 1985-86.

Sharecropping is an important aspect of the agrarian social structure of Panpara. In the 1960s and 1970s large-scale evictions of the sharecroppers took place, and now there are only 19 sharecropping households, 14 of which belong to the Scheduled Castes and Scheduled Tribes. All the sharecroppers have recorded their names under *Operation Barga*, but there is no notified or declared surplus vested land and no landless household has received any surplus vested land.

The process of agricultural modernisation has only sharpened class inequality. More than 30 per cent of the village households are now landless labourers and another 28.38 per cent are marginal cultivators owning less than 2.50 acres. In other words, more than 58 per cent of the village households form the bottom of the agrarian hierarchy.

The marginal cultivators, while representing more than 28 per cent of the total households occupy only 13.37 per cent of the total cultivable land. The small cultivators (owning land between 2.5 and 5 acres) are an important segment of the agrarian hierarchy. They represent 24.32 per cent of the households and share around 38 per cent of the total land. Middle level cultivators (owning land between 5 and 10 acres) and the big cultivators (owning more than 10 acres) represent less than 11 per cent of the households but occupy more than 48 per cent of the cultivable land (Table 5.8).

Table 5.8: Caste and Class in Panpara

Agrarian Categories by Landholding (in acres)	Upper Castes	Middle Castes	Scheduled Castes	Scheduled Tribes	Total No of Households	Landholding (in acres)
Landless A. Labourers	—	2	26	17	45 (30.41)	—
Landless B. Business and Service	3	6	—	—	9 (6.08)	—
Marginal	24	8	3	7	42	41.05

(0-2.50)					(28.38)	(13.37)
Small (2.50-5)	23	7	—	6	36 (24.32)	116.35 (37.84)
Medium (5-10)	12	—	—	—	12 (8.11)	79.67 (25.91)
Big (10+)	4	—	—	—	4 (2.70)	70.38 (22.89)
Total	66	23	29	30	148 (100.00)	307.45 (100.00)

Note : Figures in parentheses represent percentages.
Source: Intensive field survey by the author in 1985-86.

Caste and agrarian class thus coincide. While the upper stratum of the agrarian hierarchy is formed only by the upper castes, its bottom is occupied predominantly by Scheduled Caste and Scheduled Tribe households. In the category of small cultivators, there is significant representation from the upper and middle caste households, but in addition to possessing modern means of cultivation, they have potential for subsidiary means of income as well. Households of these caste groups with no lands also are either in business or in service which bring higher income. A significant number of them have invested substantially in business like transport, sale and purchase of paddy, installing paddy husking mills and also in stationery and grocery shops.

Women's Work Participation. Both caste and ethnic values and household economic compulsion have played a composite role in the extent and nature of women's work participation. The extent of work participation has changed little, but the nature of work done and work relations have changed dramatically. Female work participation rate is 36.5 per cent while for males it is 67.2 per cent (Table 5.9).

There are sharp variations in work participation rates based on caste and ethnicity. Women's work participation rate is the lowest among the upper castes, with less than 2 per cent. Among them women are found only in the teaching job, participation in agricultural and business activities being taboo, even on their own household farm.

Participation in agriculture is taboo also for the middle caste women, but they may participate in activities like small business and household industry. Women's work participation rate among them is more than 45.2

Table 5.9: Work Participation by Caste and Sex in Panpara

Caste/ Ethnic Group	Total Population		Cultivation		Agricultural Labourers		Service		Business and Household Industry		Maid Servants and Others	Total No. of Workers		Percentage to Total Female Workers
	M	F	M	F	M	F	M	F	M	F	F	M	F	F
Upper Castes	204	169 (43.4)*	76	—	5	—	12	3	35	—	—	128 (62.7)†	3 (1.8)†	2.1
Middle Castes	83	62 (16.0)	18	—	2	—	2	3	30	25	—	52 (62.6)	28 (45.2)	19.7
Scheduled Castes	90	82 (21.1)	4	—	55	18	—	—	9	22	14	68 (75.0)	54 (66.0)	38.0
Scheduled Tribes	65	76 (19.5)	6	—	43	57	—	—	—	—	—	49 (75.4)	57 (75.0)	40.2
Total	442	389 (100.0)	104	—	105	75	14	6	74	47	14	297 (76.2)	142 (36.5)	100.09

Notes: * The figures in parentheses in this column are the percentages of the women population by caste to the total women of village.
† The figures in parentheses in these columns are the male and female work participation rates i.e. percentages of the workers to the total male and female population respectively.

Source: Intensive field survey by the author in 1985-86.

per cent. Most able-bodied Tanti women of this caste group are occupied with their traditional handloom household industry, while a significant number of the Teli, Baishnav and Tambuli caste women have recently joined service and small business activities.

Women's work participation rate among the Scheduled Castes is 66 per cent while for males it is 75 per cent. Among the Scheduled Castes also, female work participation in agricultural labour is limited, because customarily not all Scheduled Caste women work in agriculture, and besides mechanisation has displaced a part of the female labour. Of the 54 working women, 22 are in small business, 14 are maidservants and 18 are agricultural labourers.

All the Scheduled Tribe women, on the other hand, are agricultural wage earners. Their high concentration in agricultural labourer category is mainly because:

(a) Their ethnic background does not become a bar to their extra-mural participation in manual work.
(b) Because they are hard working; they have not been displaced from agriculture.
(c) Because of the small size of their household landholding they are pushed to work regularly as wage earners for subsistence.
(d) They have not been able to take advantage of the new avenues of economic opportunities, because of lack of training and knowledge about available alternatives.

Women's work participation rate is highest among the Scheduled Tribes with 75 per cent in the work force and is on par with the male work participation rate.

It is seen from the above that caste value has strong association with the extent of women's work participation, the higher the social and economic status, the lower being the work participation rate. The higher caste women, who form more than 43 per cent of the female population of the village, represent only 2.3 per cent of the female work force. Women of the middle caste group, representing 16 per cent of the female population, form around 22 per cent of the work force. On the other hand, Scheduled Caste and Scheduled Tribe females while representing less than 41 per cent of the female population, form around 76 per cent of the female work force. Again the smaller the size of landholding, the higher is the extent of women's work participation.

Of the total female work force 53 per cent is in agriculture and 47 per cent is in the non-agricultural sector —business and household industry, public service and household service as maidservants.

Forms of Work Contract in Agriculture. Kaminis (female casual labourers) are the sole type of female agricultural labourers. They join work generally at around 7.30 a.m. and retire at around 6.30 p.m.with a lunch break of around two hours. A *Kamini* on an average receive Rs. 5 plus 2 kilograms of rice as her daily wage and she gets around 250 days of employment in one year. While there is no gender based wage discrimination between the *Kamini* and the *Kishan* (male casual labourers), preference is given to employing the *Kishan*. This has led to displacement of female labourers, especially of the Scheduled Castes, from agriculture. The landowners consider male labourers and tribal female labourers as swift and strong, most suited to mechanised agriculture. The landowners consider the tribal female as being *Karmatha* (laborious) and *Biswasee* (trustworthy). They have not been displaced.

Alternative Economic Activities of Women. The displaced female agricultural labourers from the Scheduled Castes have gradually shifted to alternative economic activities. Small business like paddy husking puffed rice (Muri) and Chira (flattened rice), goat-raising and poultry have been the important avenues of self-employment and alternative economic activities. These activities have good scope for expansion with the expansion of communication. For husking paddy, the traditional *Dhanki* has been replaced by paddy husking machines which a few big landowners have bought and on which the villagers can get their paddy husked on payment. The landowners also purchase the villagers rice and sell it in the urban centres. Government agencies provide loans to the villagers. For piggery and poultry the Comprehensive Area Development Project (CADP) has been extending the required facilities. A few Scheduled Caste and Scheduled Tribe women have engaged themselves intensively in these activities and have started earning a regular income. On an average a female worker earns Rs. 70 per week through such enterprise.

Scheduled Tribe women have not been able to accumulate substantial benefits out of the new economic opportunities, their economic activities being restricted to agricultural wage earning. Besides working as wage earners, they also work on their own land intensively. As agricultural labourers their bargaining capacity is very limited because of a possibility of displacement from agriculture. On the other hand, working class women who have opted for business as the mainstay of their livelihood have been experiencing a new mode of economic relations with the landowners. The economic positions of maidservants and those women workers who are attached traditionally to weaving are also different.

Political Mobilisation and Women's Response. Mobilising the vast section of the women work force who are at the bottom of the agrarian hierarchy is considered important by the leftist workers. Besides mobilising them to cast their vote in the Parliamentary, Assembly and Panchayat elections and for the implementation of *Operation Barga,* they have also organised strikes of the agricultural labourers. As there is no surplus vested land in the village, and no gender-based discrimination, the local leaders have picked up only issues like low wages and unscheduled work time.

Their efforts, however, have certainly not been a roaring success. Participation in the strikes has neither been spontaneous nor total. In July 1985, the CPI (M) party workers of the village organised a strike in the village to demand the implementation of the Minimum Wage Act, i.e. to enhance the daily wage to Rs. 14.90. The female activists of the CPI(M) led Pachimbanga Ganatantrik Mahila Samity actively campaigned for the strike and even district level leaders came to address local level meetings. But only a few Koara and Santal women, who are mainly casual labourers and landless, joined the strike, while all others kept away. When the leftist party workers warned the landowners that they would not allow them to bring any outside labour, the landowners enhanced the daily wage from Rs. 5 plus 2 kilogram rice to Rs. 5.50 plus 2 kilograms rice for all daily labourers. That brought the strike to an end.

Another strike in July 1986 for enhancement of the agricultural wage, and for implementation of the Minimum Wage Act, again, was only a partial success, joined by only a section of the tribal women. It continued for one day and ended with the enhancement of the wage rate by one rupee for the transplantation period.

While female agricultural workers of the landless families without any alternative economic activities have joined the village-level agitation, women from families with small and marginal holdings, and those who carry on business activities have shown less interest in it. Women with business interests depend on the big landowners for the marketing and loan transaction and are reluctant to spoil this relation. Women from marginal landowning and sharecropper households also have dependency relations with their landowners for modern techniques of cultivation and prefer to avoid any direct clash with the landowners.

Gofanagar

Gofanagar is agriculturally backward. Traditional tools and technology of production are prevalent here, and though since the late 1970s a few big landowners have introduced high yielding variety (HYV) seeds in crop cultivation in the absence of assured irrigation facilities, commercial and multi-crop culture have not been widespread. Small rain-fed tanks are the only source of artificial irrigation which can irrigate less than 2 per cent of the cultivable land seasonally. In the absence of potential avenue of alternative economic activities, agriculture has remained the mainstay of most of the villagers.

Agrarian Social Structure. Inequality is closely associated with the agrarian social structure of Gofanagar. Though rigorous implementation of land reform laws has led to the distribution of surplus vested land, brought the sharecroppers under *Operation Barga* and put the landholding under ceiling restriction, landholding is still concentrated among the upper castes. Even today they continue to be called *Malik* and *Babu*. The upper castes who constitute 47.5 per cent of the village households control more than 92 per cent of the cultivable land, while the Scheduled Castes and Scheduled Tribes forming 52.5 per cent of the village households control less than 8 per cent of the land. One-third of the households are landless, most of them being from the Scheduled Castes and Scheduled Tribes. The average size of landholding is small among the Scheduled Castes and Scheduled Tribes. The sharecropping system has virtually disappeared since the early 1960s (Table 5.10).

Table 5.10 : Landholding by Caste in Gofanagar (in acres)

Caste/ Ethnic Group	Percentage of Population	Households					Landholding	
		Total	Landless	Landowning	Sharecroppers	Owners of Surplus Vested Lands	Total	Average Size by Household
Upper Caste	54.69	57 (47.5)*	1	56	8	3	364.28 (92.28)*	6.51
Scheduled Castes	33.16	48 (40.0)	26	22	3	20	10.52 (2.66)	0.48

Sheduled Tribes	12.15	15 (12.5)	3	12	2	7	19.97 (5.06)	1.66
Total	100.0	120 (100.00)	30 (33.3)†	90 (66.7)†	13	30	394.77 (100.00)	4.39

Notes: *The figures in parentheses in these columns are the percentages by caste to the total household and landholding of the village respectively.
+The figures in parentheses refer to percentages.

Source: Intensive field survey by the author in 1985-86.

Sixty out of the 63 Scheduled Caste and Scheduled Tribe households are agricultural labourers and marginal cultivators, and the remaining three are small cultivators. The landless labourers and marginal cultivators represent around 62 per cent of the village households. The marginal and small cultivators while representing 50 per cent of the village households occupy only around 20 per cent of the total cultivable land.

Table 5.11: Caste and Class in Gofanagar

Agrarian Category (Landholding in acres)	Upper Castes	Scheduled Castes	Scheduled Tribes	Total No. of House-holds	Total Landholding (in acres)
Landless Labourers	1	26	3	30 (25.00)*	—
Marginal (0-2.50)	13	22	9	44 (36.67)	30.52 (7.73)*
Small (2.50-5)	13	—	3	16 (13.33)	48.97 (12.40)
Medium (5-10)	20	—	—	20 (16.67)	140.00 (35.46)
Big (10+)	10	—	—	10 (8.33)	175.28 (44.40)
Total	57	48	15	120 (100.00)	394.77 (99.99)

Note: Figures in parentheses refer to percentages.

Source: Intensive field survey by the author in 1985-86.

The medium and big landowners exclusively belong to the upper castes, and while forming 25 per cent of the village households, control around 80 per cent of the cultivable land (Table 5.11). Agrarian inequality has escalated with the sharp increase in the price of agricultural produce while agricultural wages have increased only marginally.

Women's Work Participation. The women's work participation is inversely correlated to their caste status—the higher the caste the lower the work participation, and vice versa. While the women of the upper castes constitute 52.6 per cent of the total female population, only 5.6 per cent of them are working in the extra mural sector.

Among the Scheduled Castes and Scheduled Tribes, however, two out of every three women are working (65.6 per cent and 68 per cent respectively). Poverty drives them to work, and all of them are agricultural labourers. Scheduled Caste and Scheduled Tribe women, who together form 47.4 per cent of the female population, constitute more than 94 per cent of the female work force (Table 5.12).

Forms of Work Contract. Rupini Dinmajdur is the major category of female labourers. These may be *Chara Rupini* or *Dhara Rupini.* The *Chara Rupinis* are casual labourers. On an average they get around 220 days of employment in a year. They usually join work at 8 a.m. and work up to 6.30 p.m. with a two-hour lunch break. The *Dhara Rupinis* are semi-attached to the landowners under the beck-and-call relationship. In the lean season they take a cash loan called *Kajer Upary Taka* from the landowners with the understanding that in the peak season they would work for the creditor at a daily wage rate of Re. 1 plus 2 Sers of paddy (one Ser=700 Grams) irrespective of the growing rate of wages. The cash payment is deducted at source against the loan. In 1984-85 out of the 84 female agricultural labourers 65 worked under this system.

Where the lower caste households own land, their landholding is so marginal that their womenfolk have little work there. Their efforts are more fruitfully invested in wage earning. A few Santal women work for 60 to 70 days on their own farm, and for rest of their working days they work as casual labourers. In the absence of alternative economic activity the pressure of women workers on the agrarian economy has been mounting. In contrast, the big landowners have started fishery, trading in paddy and jute and paddy husking by machine as important subsidiary sources of income. Many upper caste people have also joined government or semi-government service.

Table 5.12 : Work Participation by Caste and Sex in Gofanagar

Caste/ Ethnic Group	Total Population		Cultivation		Agricultural Labourers		Service		Business and Household Industry		Total		Percentage to Total Female Workers
	M	F	M	F	M	F	M	F	M	F	M	F	F
Upper Castes	174	141 (52.6)*	59	—	1	—	23	5	15	—	98 (56.2)†	5 (3.5)†	5.6
Scheduled Castes	92	99 (37.0)	6	—	57	65	—	—	—	—	63 (68.4)	65 (65.6)	73.0
Scheduled Tribes	42	28 (10.4)	7	—	25	19	—	—	—	—	32 (76.2)	19 (68.0)	21.4
Total	308	268 (100.0)	72	—	83	84	23	5	15	—	193 (62.7)	89 (33.2)	100.0

Notes: * The figures in parentheses in this column are the percentages of the female population by caste to the total female population of the village.

† The figures in parentheses in these columns are the percentages of the workers to the total male and female population respectively.

Source: Intensive field survey by the author in 1985-86.

Their intense dependence on agricultural wage earning has kept the female agricultural workers both socially and economically homogeneous. The basis of their homogeneity stems from the following factors :

(a) They are from the poorest section in the village.
(b) They are wage earners.
(c) They are from either the Scheduled Castes or Scheduled Tribes and carry the appellation of Chasa or Voranga (uncivilised/rustic) by the upper castes.
(d) They come under only one type of employer-employee relationship, namely the higher caste-cum-big landowners vis-a-vis the lower castes/tribe-cum-agricultural labourers.
(e) They have an identical economic interest vis-a-vis the big landowners.

In recent years, the relationship between the landowners and the female agricultural labourers has changed sharply. With the introduction of HYV paddy and large-scale commercialised jute cultivation, the demand for seasonal casual female labourers has increased for weeding of the jute fields and transplanting and harvesting paddy. Labour is in short supply in the peak seasons because outside labourers are not allowed to enter the village.

Political Mobilisation and Women's Response. Gofanagar is currently a hotbed of political mobilisation of agricultural labourers. Processions, meetings and strikes have punctuated its labour scene. In 1967 when the Leftist-dominated United Front Government came to power in West Bengal, the Communist party workers all over the state began to consolidate their mass base by mobilising the poor peasants against the big landowners. In Gofanagar, the agricultural labourers and sharecroppers repudiated all traditional relationships with the landowner. The women joined their menfolk in forcefully taking over the standing paddy from surplus vested lands which the big landowners still controlled. They also occupied ponds and gardens and seized the landowner's granary. The sharecroppers refused to part with the landowner's share of the crop. But the movement petered out with the downfall of the United Front government. Many poor peasants were arraigned on criminal charges and were under trial for a long time.

Leftist party workers have once again been mobilising the agricultural workers. This phase of mobilisation started in 1977 with the coming of the United Left Front government to power and was further consolidated in 1978 with the formation of the Gram Panchayats by the elected repesentatives of their own party members. The Revolutionary Socialist Party (RSP) workers have taken special plans to mobilise the women workers for strike. The emphasis is on women's mobilisation because :

(a) Once the women are mobilised the total household is likely to be effectively mobilised, and the strike is likely to be mass based and enduring.
(b) Women workers constitute more than half the labour force in the village.
(c) They face the maximum oppression in the labour market, being paid less for more hours of work.
(d) All women workers face the same type of problems in their working conditions.

In July 1983, the women workers organised a meeting demanding higher wages—Rs. 5 per day—and a stipulated eight hours of work. Openly giving a call for strike, they declared : "Jotedars Hoshiar" (Landowners, be careful), "Amader Majuri Barate Habe" (Enhance our wage) ; "Inquilab Zindabad", "RSP Zindabad"! The local political leaders came out openly in their support.

This was the peak season for weeding jute. Only women used to be employed for this operation for their cheap labour and for their skill. The landowners pooh-poohed the strike, but most of the women workers joined it though the males joined the work. The anxious landowners tried to cajol individual labourers, but in vain. In the evening, they arranged a meeting with the labour leaders and enhanced the wage from Rs. 2 to Rs. 3 plus breakfast. The strike was then withdrawn.

In the Parliamentary election of 1984, the RSP candidate of this constituency (Balurghat) was re-elected. In the election manifesto he had promised higher wages to the agricultural labourers and that promise had to be made good. The local leaders organised the women workers for a strike on 31 December 1984, which every single agricultural working woman of the village joined. They demanded:

(a) Implementation of the Minimum Wage Act to give Rs. 14.90 as daily wage to all categories of labourers.
(b) No gender-based discrmination.
(c) Stipulated 8 hours of works in a day.
(d) Extra wages for overtime work.
(e) For the *Basarmarus* (permanent farm servants) one month paid holiday in a year.

It was the paddy harvesting season. For two days the landowners got their work done by the male workers, migrant labourers and labourers from neighbouring villages. But on the third day the males joined their womenfolk in the strike and strongly objected to the entry of outside labourers in the village. The landowners, in a way intimidated, gave up their attempt to hire labour from outside. Every passing day was increasing the hardship of the strikers. Many of them went to work under government contractors far away from the village. Many sold their small store of livestock like ducks and goats to save the family from starvation.

On the eighth day of the strike the landowners buckled up. They arranged a meeting with the labourers where it was decided that :

(a) Women workers would be given Rs. 2 plus 3.5 Sers of paddy as daily wage instead of Re. 1 plus 3.5 Sers of paddy. The wage for male casual labourers was fixed at Rs. 3 plus 3.5 Sers of paddy. Breakfast would be given for all casual labourers as usual.
(b) Women workers would join work at 8 a.m. and would retire at 6.30 p.m. with a break for around two and a half hours.
(c) The Jhis (maidservants) would be given Rs. 15 as part time monthly wage. (Their primarily work as agricultural labourers.)
(d) The male labourers would join work at 7.30 a.m. and work till 6.30 p.m. with a break for lunch for around two hours.
(e) The *Basarmaru* would be given Rs. 45 plus 2.5 Manns (1 Mann = 28 Kg.) of paddy as monthly salary and an extra one month (30 days) holiday with full payment.
(f) The *Masara* (monthly workers) would be given Rs. 50 plus 2.5 Manns of paddy as monthly salary.
(g) All groups concerned including the political party workers

would take the initiative to maintain congenial relations between the employers and employees in the village.

These decisions were documented and hailed by the labourers. This strike was a revealing lesson in that :

(a) It proved the organisational strength of the female labourers.
(b) It highlighted the causes of immediate discontent of the labourers.
(c) It institutionalised strike and agricultural labourers' agitation at the village level.
(d) It exposed the weakenesses of the landowners vis-a-vis the collective strength of the labourers.

The victorious women, however, had to pay the cost of their victory in the lean season. When they went to the landowners to have *Kajer Uparay Taka* (advance loan), many were refused and told satirically

"Go to the leaders.
They wil give you the loan. They will feed you."

The pay-off for the women came again during the next peak season of transplantation. In the first week of July 1985 they called for another strike demanding full implementation of the Minimum Wage Act. For the farmer, every passing day in the transplantation operation is of critical importance. The landowners put male workers on the job, but they were neither enough nor skilled. After two days of the strike the landowners made a settlement with the women workers. They enhanced their wage to Rs. 3.50 plus 2 Sers of rice.(Many landowners privately outbid each other, paying Rs. 4 plus 2 Sers of rice as wage.)

It is extremely significant that the leadership of this strike came from the women workers. They organised processions and meetings by themselves. A Santal woman from a neighbouring village gave a lively speech. Other women joined her in chanting, "Inquilab Zindabad," "Amader Dabi Mante Habe" (Recognise demands). It was also the first time that the landowners directly negotiated with the women workers. Clearly, a distinct leadership was emerging from among the women workers.

SECTION III

THE EMERGING TRENDS : THE FACETS OF COMMONALITIES AND DIFFERENCES

The villages under study have had varying levels of economic development and agricultural modernisation and rate of social change. Khanpur and Shalgeriya, which experienced vehement peasant movements in 1946-47 and 1967-71 respectively, have undergone two distinct processes of economic formation and social change. While Khanpur has been introduced to rapid economic development, agricultural modernisation and occupational diversification, Shalgeriya stagnates with agricultural backwardness, poverty and occupational and economic insecurity. The ill-assorted economic formations of these two villages extend across larger society and state of West Bengal as well. Both within the Northern and Southern regions of West Bengal and between the villages under study these distinctions are clearly seen. Comparing and contrasting the socio-economic formations of Khanpur and Shalgeriya with Panpara in South Bengal and Gofanagar in North Bengal, we discover striking similarities and differences in terms of economic and political formations in general and women's response to political mobilisation in particular (See Chart 5.1).

Khanpur and Panpara are put under category 'A'. Though these two villages belong to two different regions of West Bengal, they possess some important common economic and political features. These are (a) high rate of economic development, (b) high rate of agricultural modernisation, (c) high rate of occupational diversification, and (d) low rate and partial participation of women in political mobilisation. While Khanpur has a vehement peasant movement background, Panpara is devoid of such experience. Shalgeriya and Gofanagar are put under category 'B' since they have some important similarities in terms of (a) low rate of economic development, (b) low rate of agricultural modernisation, (c) low rate of occupational diversification, and (d) high rate and total participation of working-class women in response to political mobilisation. These similarities have emerged in spite of regional differences between these villages and the fact that while Shalgeriya has a peasant movement background, Gofanagar has not.

Against this diversified backdrop, the social relationships of the working-class women with the major social groups interacting in these

Chart 5.1 : Similarities and Differences between Khanpur, Shalgeriya, Panpara and Gofanagar

Category of Village	Name of Village	Region	Rate of Economic Development	Extent of Agricultural Modernisation	Extent of Occupational Diversification	Whether having a Peasant Movement Background	Exent of Women's Political Response to Collective Mobilisation
A	Khanpur	North Bengal	High	High	High	Tebhaga Movement 1946-47	Low/Partial
	Panpara	South Bengal	Very High	Very High	High	No	Low/Partial
B	Shalgeriya	South Bengal	Low	Low	Low	Naxalite Movement 1967-71	High/Total
	Gofanagar	North Bengal	Low	Low	Very Low	No	High/Total

villages have been diverse. The commonalities in social relationships within the same category of villages and the differences with other category of villages are delineated in Chart 5.2

Among the primordial groups, major differences in social relationships have emerged with kinsmen/kinswomen and own caste/tribal group members. In the 'B' category villages the working-class women's social relationships with these social groups are cohesive, deriving from a common economic background and occupational foundation. On the other hand, in the 'A' category village their social relationships with these social groups are competitive. They compete among themselves for deriving more benefits out of the new economic opportunities and for getting more employment. Their competitive relationship is tied up with their occupational and economic interest.

Relationships with family members in both categories, though integrated, display small differences in terms of the typology of the family. In the 'B' category villages the families of the working-class women are entirely nuclear ; in the 'A' category villages there are 12.5 per cent joint families.

In both categories of villages, social relationships between the villagers are disintegrated. But there are some important differences between the two categories of villages. In the 'B' category villages disintegration has been manifested vis-a-vis occupational interests against the other occupational groups (landowners and moneylenders). In contrast, in the 'A' category villages the disintegrated social relationships have spread all over the village across the primordial and occupational groups.There are contradictory economic interest among members of the working-class women themselves and between the various occupational groups as well.

In the 'B' category villages relationships between the female agricultural labourers and agricultural labourers' group as a whole are of solidarity. This solidarity has its basis in common economic background. They exert the force of the solidarity against the landowners-cum-traditional moneylenders of the village in pressurising them to enhance the wage rates, etc. They are frequently mobilised against the landowners for political action. They openly describe the landowners as *Shosok-kari* (class of exploiters). Since there have not emerged any potential avenues of alternative economic activities, they have only an indifferent relationship with the businessmen.

In category 'A' villages, on the other land, the female workers have competitive/disintegrated relationships with the female agricultural labourers and the agricultural lábour group as a whole. The disintegration

Chart 5.2 : Nature of Social Relationships of the Agricultural Working-Class Women in the A and B Category Villages

	Major Social Groups	Villages Under Category B	Village Under Category A
1.	Primordial Groups		
	(a) Family Members	Integrated	Integrated
	(b) Kinsmen/Kinswomen	Cohesive	Competitive
	(c) Caste/Tribal Group Members	Cohesive	Competitive
	(d) Villagers	Disintegrated	Disintegrated
2.	Occupational Groups		
	(a) Female Agricultural Labourers	United	Competitive/Disintegrated
	(b) Agricultural Labourers Group as a Whole	United	Competitive/Disintegrated
	(c) Landowners-cum-Traditional Moneylenders	Conflicting	Contractual and Purposive
	(d) Businessmen/Purchasers	Indifferent	Entrepreneurial
3.	Government Machinery/Development Agencies		
	(a) Police/Administration	Aggressive	Submissive
	(b) Bank, BDO, CADP, etc.	Indifferent	Transactional/Enterprising
4.	Professional Groups		
	(a) Political Workers	Receptive	Selective Receptivity
	(b) Adult School Instructors	——	Initiative

has been marked by the emergence of various occupational sub-categories among them, by displacement of a section of female agricultural labourers and by their partial participation in the agricultural workers' agitation. Their relationship with the agricultural labourer groups as a whole has also been "competitive": they compete among themselves for more economic gain and employment.

Because occupational diversification has taken place in category 'A' villages, the female agricultural workers have got economic relationships not only with the landowners in their economic nexus but also with businessmen as an important occupational group. Their relationships with the landowners have been "contractual" and "purposive". The majority of the female agricultural workers of these villages enter into open contractual work relations with the landowners. Their extra-contractual work relationships with the landowners have been "purposive" in getting plough, cattle, etc. from them to cultivate their own small plots of land. Their relationship with the businessmen/purchasers has been "entrepreneurial". They maintain a calculative behaviour with them. They also take the risk of investing their small savings in small businesses. The labour market of these villages has obviously a greater degree of market economy. This is a major structural shift in the traditional agrarian economy. The social relations of the female workers here are widely influenced by the market forces rather than by traditional values and norms.

The development of alternative avenues of employment has enhanced importance of Rural Development Banks, Block Development Office, Comprehensive Area Development Project, etc. in category 'A' villages. The government machinery and development agencies have been widely accepted by the villagers. Women workers maintain "transactional and enterprising" relationships with these institutions. Many of them have taken loans for agriculture and business from these institutions and maintain regular contact with them. In 'B' category villages no elaborate network of these agencies has come into being and the women workers are indifferent towards these agencies. In recent years they have developed an antagonistic attitude towards the visiting police force. Many a time they have united against the arrest of members of their own occupational group. In villages under category 'A' female workers have a "submissive" attitude towards the police force.

Political workers have been important components of the professional groups in the rural society of West Bengal. In the 'B' category villages, in the process of their mobilisation against the landowners the female workers have been receptive to the political party workers. They are mobilised by the latter with the ideology of rapid social change. In the 'A' category villages, on the other hand, the nature of their relationship with the political workers has been of selective receptivity. They follow only those directions which appear suitable for their economic interest. Here only a small section of the working-class women respond to the call of the political party workers regularly.

The female instructors of the Adult Education Centre have been the most important professional group members of the female workers in the 'A' category villages. The working-class women's relationship with these instructors have been imitative. The female instructors are from the higher caste families of these villages. The women who are enrolled in these educational centres try to follow the overt life-style of the instructors. They also seek the cooperation of the instructors in purchasing dresses, cosmetics, etc. from the urban centres. They follow the suggestions of these instructors pertaining to health and child care very carefully. In the 'B' category villages there is no Adult Education Centre.

The emerging patterns of social relationships that have been manifested in these two categories of villages have been closely intertwined with the ideology of the contemporary political mobilisation on the one hand, and the broad socio-economic formations of the villages, on the other. They have produced a distinct pattern of collective mobilisation in the villages under reference. In the next chapter we shall explain the major facets of the change and continuity in the form and direction of women's response to collective mobilisations/movements and provide an explanation of this change and continuity.

VI

PATTERNS OF WOMEN'S RESPONSE TO COLLECTIVE MOBILISATION : COMPARISON AND ANALYSIS

The nature of the peasantry's collective mobilisation has significantly changed in West Bengal over the years. Indeed, sharp diversities have emerged in the phenomenon in the interim between extensive peasant movements on the one hand, and the contemporary period, on the other. The form and extent of women's response to these processes of collective mobilisation also have been diverse. In this chapter we shall explain the major trends of collective mobilisation in West Bengal and analyse the form and direction of women's response to it.

Patterns of Women's Response : Diachronic Perspective. Though there have been certain differences between the Tebhaga Movement of 1946-47 and the Naxalite Movement of 1967-71 in the direction, methodology of action and form of collective mobilisation, the nature and extent of women's response in these movements shows a fascinating uniformity. The radicalism of the Leftist party leadership introduced women of the villages under the Tebhaga and Naxalite movements to the non-institutionalised process of mobilisation. Women were offered an unprecedented opportunity to participate in full measure in these movements. The introduction of the radical and non-institutionalised mode of mobilisation led to a break with the normative structure and traditional mode of social relationships. The whole gamut of the social network which had been operating apparently within the context of primordial loyalties of neighbourhood, caste, kinship and family experienced a tremendous transformation in this period.

The radicalised and non-institutionalised political mobilisation has now been replaced by institutionalised parliamentary party politics. The Leftist political parties, who once sponsored radicalism and militancy to mobilise the peasantry for collective action in the extensive peasant movements, are now concerned with the legislative processes and electoral politics. The United Left Front Government which came to power in 1977 has been advocating mass mobilisation for the rigorous implementation of land reform laws, for improving the economic conditions of the rural poor and to destroy the bases of feudalism in the countryside. Collective action has thus been institutionalised. The process of women's mobilisation is defined and directed within institutionalised perspectives of the political parties, the states and the society.

The major trends of political mobilisation of working-class rural women in these two periods (extensive peasant movement and contemporary) under reference are given in Chart 6.1.

Chart 6.1: Trends of Mobilisation of Women Agricultural Workers in the Extensive Peasant Movement and in the Contemporary Period

	Extensive Peasant Movement Period	Contemporary Period
1.	Aggressive, hostile without immediate limit.	Aggressiveness and hostility are limited within given direction.
2.	Breaking old norms and values.	Importance to selected norms and values.
3.	Guided by the ideology of radical social change and vehement shift of the economic orders.	Guided by institutionalised ideology of social change, and change in the economic order has been perceived as a gradual process.
4.	Attempt to elevate economic status following political path.	Attempt to elevate economic status following diversified occupational path.

5.	Organised by secret organisations and partially open organisations.	Organised by open and recognised organisations.
6.	Collective action and total and spontaneous mobilisation at one point of time and uncalculative.	Mostly sectorial action and specific mobilisation from time to time and calculative.
7.	Fought for mostly the unrecognised demands, the immediate enemy being the big landowners.	Pressurising the landowners and government bureaucrats to implement the recognised and institutionalised demands.
8.	Followed the strategy of attacking the landowners, the police, cutting the standing paddy of the land owners forcibly and helping the underground rebel.	Following strikes, processions and negotiations.
9.	Faced domination by government authorities and police force.	Getting encouragement by the political parties in power.

Patterns of Women's Response: Synchronic Perspective. Though the contemporary process of institutionalisation of political mobilisation has superseded radicalism and militancy across the state irrespective of levels of social and political formations, women's response to collective mobilisation has been uneven. The major trends of their response can be classified under 'A' and 'B' category of villages referred to earlier (See Chart 6.2).

Chart 6.2: Varied Trends of Women's Response to Collective Mobilisation Between 'A' and 'B' Category Villages

	'B' Category Villages	'A' Category Villages
1.	The agricultural working-class women of these villages are highly politically mobilised and they are receptive to the political ideas of rapid social change.	Only a section of women of these villages are politically mobilised and receptive to the political ideas of rapid social change.
2.	The female workers are following the political path to elevate their socio-economic status.	Majority of the female workers are following diversified economic path to elevate their socio-economic status.
3.	In the agricultural workers' agitation most female agricultural workers participate.	In the agricultural workers' agitation only a section of the female agricultural workers participate.
4.	Their participation in collective mobilisation is total, spontaneous and frequent.	Their participation in collective mobilisation is sporadic, non-spontaneous and occasional.
5.	There is unidirectional relationship between the landowners and the female workers in terms of employer-employee relationship. The whole gamut of this relationship is politicised.	There are multi-directional relationships between the landowners and the female workers in terms of agriculture, business and household industry, etc. activities. Only one aspect of their relationship tends to be politicised.

Women's Response: An analytical Perspective: Both historically and in the contemporary period rural women's response to collective mobilisation has thus been diverse. These diversities are to be understood in reference to the dynamics of the ideology of the peasant movements, broad processes of social formation and the interplay of various endogenous and exogenous forces thereon. Conventional theories alone cannot explain it satisfactorily. Against the given empirical backdrop we have developed an analytical perspective to categorise the peasant movement based on its ideological orientation and form of collective mobilisation. This categorisation will help us understand the dynamic of rural women's response to collective mobilisation, the position of women within given socio-economic formation and the interplay of composite social forces on them.

Based on the concepts of social movements given by various scholars (Blumer 1951, Toch 1965, Haberle 1972, Gusfield 1972, Wilson 1973), we perceive a peasant movement as organised efforts of the poor peasants and agricultural working class (including agricultural labourers, sharecroppers, tenants and subsistence cultivators) to bring changes in the patterns of the ownership, control and use of land, share of the agricultural produce between the sharecroppers and landowners, agricultural wage structure, etc. through collective mobilisation.

Ideology, organisation, leadership, strategy and tactics are crucial elements of a movement and these tend to change over a period of time. Long-lasting social movements sooner or later become routinised. Many social movements start off with radical ideology but develop their own establishment in turn. Movements which reject the existing institutions will in turn attempt to codify the belief system and provide institutionalised arrangement to ensure its code of conduct (Rao 1978 : 3-10; 193:251).

The ideology and organisation of the extensive peasant movements have undergone phenomenal changes in course of time. These changes have obvious bearings on the form and direction of the peasantry's mobilisation in general and the direction of the movement towards change in particular. Peasant movements that began with non-institutionalised form of and radical direction to mass mobilisation are guided by the radical anti-establishment ideology of rapid change in the agrarian social structure. Breaking up of traditional and established norms, values, customs and institutions has been their agenda. Though based on the broad economic formation and socio-cultural context of society the life-span of such radical movements has been varied, their intensive periods of actions and mass mobilisation having been short-lived.

Where peasant movements are manifested in terms of institutionalised mass mobilisation the whole gamut of mobilisation is codified, and recognised. Guided by the reformative ideology of social change, in course of collective mobilisation they get old institutions, norms, values and customs redefined in the new context. These reformative movements have longer life-span. A reformative peasant movement resorts to institutionalised mass mobilisation guided by the ideology of gradual change in certain selected institutional arrangements of society. Radical and reformative social movements are not necessarily opposed to each other; rather one may become an extension of the other over time.

The Tebhaga and Naxalite movements were radical peasant movements while contemporary peasant mobilisation is reformative. In the former, non-institutionalised mobilisation of peasantry took off from the radical Marxist and Marxist-Maoist-Leninist ideologies of social change. They took to unrecognised methods like forcibly occupying the land and cutting the standing paddy from the fields of landowners, waging war against the landowners and the police force. The Naxalite Movement went even further with its line of annihilation of Jotedars (the big landowners). In the Tebhaga Movement was heard for the first time the slogan "Langal jar jamin tar" (land to the tiller), signifying the peasantry's proprietorship. It was a radical movement in the context of the social realities of the time, and discarded the traditional norms, values, institutions and the broad normative structure of society.

A radical movement proclaims a strong protest ideology against social and economic inequality. The Tebhaga Movement began under the auspices of the Bengal Kisan Sabha, and the Naxalite Movement under the broad Marxist-Leninist-Maoist ideological perspective of a breakaway radical group of the Communist Party of India (Marxist) who in 1969 formed the Communist Party of India (Marxist-Leninist). The ideology of both organisations stood for an egalitarian social order. Rapid social change and basic alterations in the normative and institutional framework of society were to be brought about through rapid mobilisation of the rural folk.

In the contemporary reformative peasant movement, the peasantry is mobilised by the recognised political parties following institutionalised norms and procedures. The political parties may be of diverse ideological pursuits. In the women's mobilisation, the non-institutionalised militancy and hostility that the peasant women showed in radical peasant movements have declined, the primary concern now being the securing of legislative gains for women (Basu 1981:22).

The Leftist parties, especially the CPI, CPI (M), RSP and others have "revised" their ideology. From an intractable position of non-participation in elections and a total debunking of parliamentary institutions the Central Committee of the Communist Party of India, Marxist-Leninist (CCCPI-ML) itself identified with the leadership of Satya Narain Sinha and opted for participation in the Assembly election of 1977. The party stated categorically that "violence is not our ideology, our ideology is

Marxism-Leninism" (cf. Mukherjee 1983: 55).

The potential of the ideology of a peasant movement to provide opportunities to rural women to exhibit their accumulated discontent as members of the deprived section of society and as women determine their response to it. The response of working-class rural women has been more obvious, spontaneous and total to radical movements than to reformative ones. The former gave them wide scope to manifest their accumulated discontent with their stress on rapid social change and drastic overhauling of the normative and institutional arrangements of society. The reformative peasant movements on the other hand, with their stress on "revisionism" of ideologies and gradual social change, reinforce in one form or another, the norms and institutions that either legitimise or promote the cause of deprivation among women.

Basis of Accumulated Deprivation Syndrome: The accumulated deprivation syndrome arises out of the composite social situation. This situation is related to the traditional values of the caste hierarchy and patriarchy, low access of women to literacy, property and health facilities, gender-based wage discrimination, economic insecurity and subjugation and marginalisation in society.

Women's participation in extra-mural manual agricultural activities is a matter of social sentiment. The supply of female labour in the said activities would depend largely on the caste and community composition of the village and the traditional behaviour pattern associated with it (Gadgil 1965:9). Women labourers of West Bengal are invariably drawn from the lower caste or ethnic backgrounds, and are called *Chotolok* or *Chasha* women by the *Bhadralok or Babus* (the big landowning-cum-higher caste people). Economic deprivation has accentuated their social deprivation. Predominantly from the marginal peasant, sharecropper and landless labourer households, they occupy the bottom of the agrarian hierarchy. Socio-cultural and economic factors are integrally correlated to women's seclusion or independence, which in turn contributes to their political passivity or independence. The mutually reinforcing nature of cultural and economic factors suggests why Scheduled Caste and Tribal women agricultural labourers have everywhere been more likely to engage in protest than other women (Basu 1981: 295-97). The greater work participation of Dalit and Adivasi women reflects the fact that these groups are highly concentrated in the lowest agricultural positions. Dalit and tribal women are crucial to organising agricultural labour and generally are the most militant section (Omvedt 1977: 381-82). Their militancy arises out of their social and economic deprivation which is legitimised by institutionalised norms and values of society.

At the village level female agricultural workers are subjected to dominant upper caste values. The traditional values of the village perceive women as *Grihalaxmi* (Goddess of Wealth of the house), but not the female agricultural workers whose nature of work is derogatory and demeaning in terms of upper caste values. Their activities and economic conditions are justified in terms of the doctrine of *Karma* by the upper caste landowning groups.

Again, patriarchy is a social fact. India is predominantly a society ruled by an ideology of female subordination, patrilocal families with the economic controls (of land, capital, and the labour processes of women and children) firmly in male hands (Bardhan 1985: 2207). The Scheduled Caste, Scheduled Tribe and ex-tribal women of rural India are still dominated by upper caste patriarchic values. They have little or no participation and representation in the decision-making processes both at home and outside; familial, communal or societal issues are usually decided without their participation. Patriarchal behavioural norms and values imposing enormous restrictions on women's regular interaction, conditioning them to tolerate injustice silently both in the family and in the workplace. These values also contribute enormously to women's low access to literacy, medical facilities and productive resources.

Working-class women are bereft of minimum economic security. Being members of the lowest section of the agrarian society they are subjected to all kinds of exploitation and hardships along with their male family members.

Wage discrimination, unspecified work schedule, extra economic coercion are inseparable from their work norms. In everyday life, together with their male family members they experience the end product of economic deprivation in terms of illiteracy, ill health, starvation, poverty and frustrations. Frequently they erupt in gender-based manifestation in the family as physical violence and wife-beating. Truly, a low caste woman's life is drudgery.

The composition of these dominant caste value, patriarchy and the economic foundation of society are widely responsible for the accumulated deprivation syndrome of rural women.

The economic foundation of society subjugates and discriminates against the agricultural working-class woman, while the dominant caste and social values provide a broad normative framework to exclude her from the mainstream of social life. Patriarchy reinforces the social and economic inequalities and marginalisation of women in the family and society.

Radical Peasant Movements and Women's Discontent: Radical peasant movements challenged the normative arrangement of society that legitimised the oppression and marginalisation of rural working-class women. Though their ideologies did not focus entirely on matters concerning rural women, they gave them scope to fight against gender-based social and economic injustice. They joined the struggle against the big landowners and fought for social issues, but to these toiling women these ideologies had an appeal which went beyond class struggle. They saw an opportunity not only to improve their economic lot, but also to break loose from the bondage of the age-old normative structure of society and the control of patriarchy. These movements provided them ample opportunity to slacken the patriarchal control, and their response was spontaneous, hostile, aggressive and total. In the radical process of mobilisation, it was for the first time that they stood side by side with men publicly and got the taste of equal responsibility and status at all stages of its development. They were encouraged for total mobilisation against those who exploited them over the years and also to revolt against the social order that legitimised their low social status.

For these toiling women, it was not simply a response to the exigencies of society; nor was it merely an organised effort to improve their deteriorating economic condition. To them it was widely a response to the promise of an egalitarian society, a response to the collective mobilisation which aimed to bring radical change in the old values, norms and institutions of their society. As in the Telengana struggle also, women poured into these movements 'seizing eagerly an opportunity that opened up the possibility to respond to a world in which they were hitherto powerless and invisible' (Kannabiran and Lalitha 1989).

These movements brought a qualitative change in their perception. This perception did not sprout among them mechanically and instantaneously : it was a gradual process. While within the existing socio-economic realities of life women had increasing awareness of their accumulated deprivation, the aspiration for equality and a vehement change in the old order were mediated by the ideological appeal of these movements and the process of mass mobilisation. While the men viewed their actions as an onslaught on the exploitative terms and conditions of work and an attempt to bring a better condition of life, the women saw their own actions as being, in addition, a fervant attempt to sever the age-old societal and familial bondages and subjugations which they experienced as females. They found in their action an aspiration for equality both in the family and in society.

Some of the participants of the Tebhaga and Naxalite Movements have given voice to this insight. Fulo Kamaini, an illiterate widow, above 60 years old, narrates her experience of the Tebhaga Movement:

> We were sharecroppers of the Singhabahiri Zamindar of the village. We had no time, no life, no identity of our own. From sunrise to sunset, all the year round, we worked either in the field or in the house of the landowner. Being a woman of a sharecropper family, I was to work under compulsory Begar (working in the field only receiving food) in the field of the landowner frequently. Again, I was to look after some of the household chores there regularly only receiving breakfast.
>
> But, there I was made to realise that I was a low caste woman. I was not supposed to touch towels, dry clothes, water, not to go towards the inner parts of the house. We were always made to feel that we were unimportant, because we were women. Both in the home and in the village we were told to show respect to the higher caste people by maintaining distance from them and by maintaining *Ghomta* (Purdah) regularly. We were taught not to ignore or show disrespect to them in spite of all their misconduct. Even if they deprived us of our daily wage we were supposed to tolerate it silently. We were not supposed to speak loudly or to laugh in front of them.
>
> I came to know about the Tebhaga through my husband. Initially they were talking about the *Shoson* (exploitation) of the landowners. As the movement started growing we were given more and more responsibilities—cooking food for the activists, providing facilities for the secret meetings, receiving and giving messages. Gradually the leaders started listening to us (women). They started consulting us in most matters. We were given some importance. We were invited. We came to the street ignoring all the *Prathas* (norms). We experienced a flood which washed away all the *Purano Niyam Canuns* (old traditions and customs) of society and tortures of the landowners.

When asked why she jumped into that flood, she replied : '*For a Baro Paribartan* (great change)".

For Nagenbala, a participant in the Naxalite Movement, the movement was

> a wildfire to burn all the old discriminatory customs, rules and systems. We participated in this movement to bring a new *Samaj Babastha* (social order). Our struggle was not only against the class of landowners, but was also against the system. During the struggle we could deny the bondages which enslaved women in society. As we involved ourselves with the movement, new horizons of hope opened to us.

Reformative Peasant Movement and Women's Discontent. In contemporary reformative movement working-class women have very limited scope to unveil their latent discontent.

The mobilisations are focused only on bringing reformative changes in society. Various legislative measures have been undertaken to advance this aim, and the vehicle of mass mobilisation used to ensure their implementation.

The Left Front governments have given prime importance for implementing land reform laws. The United Front government (Left-dominated) which came to power in 1967 took possession of land legally declared surplus (vested land) from the *Jotedars* and distributed it among the landless poor. "Get the list of vested lands and take possession by yourselves", they were told. About 2.5 lakh acres of land were distributed to about equal number of peasants. The Left Front government which came to power in 1977 considered land reform as the cornerstone of the rural development strategy. The main features of this can be summarised as follows :

(a) Quick recording of the name of Bargadars (sharecroppers) through *Operation Barga* and thereby securing to them legal rights.

(b) Distribution of already available ceiling-surplus vested land among the landless and poor rural workers in active cooperation with the Panchayati Raj institutions.

(c) Dictating and vesting more ceiling-surplus land, through quasi-judicial investigative machinery with the help of the rural workers' organisations and Panchayati Raj institutions.

(d) Giving coverage of institutional credit to sharecroppers and assignees of vested land in order to irreversibly snap the bondage with the landlords and moneylenders.

(e) Assigning permanent title to all landless agricultural workers for homestead purposes (including sharecroppers, artisans and fishermen) who are occupying others' land up to 0.99 acres.

(f) Providing small sources of irrigation to assignees of vested lands with heavy subsidy from the state.

(g) Giving financial assistance in the form of subsidies to the poor peasants.

(h) Excepting the small and marginal farmers from the revenue.

(i) Restoration of alienated land which had been lost by poor and marginal farmers through distress sale, provided the purchaser himself was not a poor peasant with landholding less than one acre.

(j) Designing the Food for Work Programme in order to develop rural infrastructure which would benefit primarily the assignees of vested land and marginal farmers...(Government of West Bengal 1980).

The wage of the agricultural labourers was raised to Rs. 14.90 in 1977 from the existing Rs. 8.10 (W.B. Agricultural Wage Act, 1977). Movements have been initiated to implement the prescribed wages. In fact, the law which has been enacted for a minimum wage is the outcome of the struggle by the agricultural workers under the leadership of Leftist peasant organisations (Bose 1981: 2054-55).

To implement this programme the Leftist workers, through their mass organisation, have been mobilising the peasantry. The village Panchayats which are dominated by the Leftists, have been given prime importance to carry on day-to-day mobilisation of the agricultural workers and to carry out the Left Front government's decisions at the grassroots level.

Women's organisations also have come forward to organise working-class women for collective mobilisation. All major political parties in West Bengal have their women's front: Pradesh Congress Mahila Samiti, (Congress), Nikhil Banga Mahila Sanga (RSP), Mahila Sanskritik Sangha (SUCI), Agragami Mahila Samiti (FB), Mahila Samiti (CPI) and Pachimbanga Ganatantrik Mahila Samiti (CPI(M)). The proliferation of women's organisations indicates the increasing awareness of women on contemporary social and political issues. All of them have undertaken elaborate programmes to mobilise women for collective action under their banners. The women's wing of the CPI(ML) (Satya Narain Sinha—Santosh Rana group) since 1977 has adopted an elaborate programme for women's liberation movement and promised to organise women for uninterrupted mass movement.

A scrutiny of the activities of the United Left Front government shows that though the class interests of the lowest section of the agrarian society are well represented in its rural development programmes, specific women's issues and interests are not adequately reflected there.

The class positions of the rural male and female workers are not always the same since they have different terms and conditions of work resulting from their different positions in the labour market. The class position of the household does not necessarily represent the class position of the women workers.

The West Bengal government makes the claim of having been highly successful in upholding the class interest of the rural poor by implementing the land reform laws especially through *Operation Barga* and distribution of surplus vested land. It merits examination how working-class women's interests have been taken care of in terms of their access to property in these programmes.

Operation Barga is a massive programme to record the names of sharecroppers. It started in September 1977. The Left Front government has attached utmost importance and urgency to recording names of Bargadars for two reasons. First, once the name of the Bargadars is recorded the owner will not be able to evict them; and secondly, the recorded Bargadars are entitled to have institutional facilities (Chattopadhyay 1979). In 1977, 2,42,000 sharecroppers were brought under *Operation Barga*. In 1984 their numbers rose up to 12,79,940 (Government of West Bengal 1985:13). Our study shows that in all the four villages studied all the sharecroppers have been brought under *Operation Barga*. But in spite of the active role of women in agrarian struggles and the notion of equality among the sexes adopted by the Left Front the tenures of landholding have been recorded invariably in the name of the male members of the household. Again the tenure of sharecropping is inherited by the male members mostly. Indeed, the widows and daughters of the deceased sharecroppers have been deprived of their dues. The institutional facilities given by the government too are received by the male members of the sharecropper household.

Distribution of surplus vested land is another important objective of the land reform policy. Since 1977, the process of distribution of surplus vested land has been smoothed in West Bengal. Till 1977, there were 11,22,000 acres of surplus vested land of which 6,12,000 acres were distributed among 9,63,000 landless people. In 1983 a total of 12,63,000 acres of land were declared surplus vested and till February 1985, 7,70,000 acres of land were distributed among 15,00,000 landless people (Govt. of W.B., 1985: 13).

Most of the certification of surplus vested lands (Pattas) however, are issued in the name of the male members of the family even though the distribution of surplus vested lands came into being as a result of the struggle of both men and women in these villages. Of the 197 persons allotted surplus vested lands in these four villages, only five are female.

Institutional loan has been another important aspect of the rural economy in recent years. As many as 95.5 per cent of the institutional loans to the villages under reference are granted in the name of the male members of the household. Issues pertaining to the women's insignificant access to property have been ignored by political party activists. Though the political parties have shown progressive attitudes in mobilising women for collective action, they have lacked the initiative to take concrete action for the empowerment of rural women. Recording the tenure of the share-croppers under *Operation Barga*, distribution of surplus vested land and providing institutional loans in the joint names of male and female, or proportionately in the name of male and female could have been an important instrument for the socio-economic empowerment of working-class rural women. But in the absence of any political commitment of the parties in power to these issues, this may remain a distant hope.

The ideology of contemporary peasant movement envisages very limited potential for women's liberation. Following the tactical path of partial ideological modification and revisionism, the contemporary reformative movement has reinforced the old institutions in new form. Hence, there has been gender-based role stereotyping for working-class rural women within the normal functioning of society. Women have been left with little scope to challenge the bondage of the normative structure, the control of patriarchy and the economic discrimination and subsequent marginalisation.

Socialisation and Gender-Role Stereotyping. Gender roles are transmitted through the values and norms of various agencies of socialisation. Family is the basic unit of socialisation of its members. In the process of transmitting norms, values, customs and traditions of society, the family reinforces the traditional patriarchic values of women's subjugation in the world-view of its members. The structuring of women as gendered subject through Hindu rituals and practices is fundamentally implied in the constitution and reproduction of a social system characterised by the subordination of women (Dube 1988: 181). The process of socialisation is closely interlinked with the proceses of sexual division of labour in the family and in society. The broad perspective of the work norm is shaped within this process. The process of socialisation has acted counter to the idea of equal status and role of women in society. Working-class women have been socialised not only to bear the burden of mounting household chores, but also to accept the discriminatory work conditions in society. They have also been socialised to tolerate even extreme forms of drudgery, and unquestioningly accept the outbursts of the rage of the malefolk manifested in physical violence. Any resistance against these inculcated norms of society is severely criticised. Parbati, a 38-year-old Scheduled Caste woman reacting to the physical violence of her husband points out:

> Since in reply to his (husband's) physical assault I gave him a simple push to protect myself, all the elder members of the family stopped talking to me. It has become the gossip of the village. Even the little children started commenting that I was a *Madda* (masculine). I have been criticised in the family, in the street, in the market, in the village. . . everywhere.

Regarding paid employment and household chores she says:

> The Sun will start rising in the West if the malefolk start washing clothes, cleaning utensils and the house, collecting firewood and fetching drinking water regularly. These are meant for us. But, why should we not do all these things? Even if we starve we are not allowed to work as *Khetmajdur* (casual agricultural labourers). What work we are to do and how to do it are decided by the *Samaj* (society) and my *Vater* (husband).

Parbati's expression is typical of the feelings and experiences of the majority of the women workers across the society. It clearly depicts the aspects of gender role stereotyping in the rural areas and its perpetuation of individual women's resistance. The normative structure of society and the caste values define the behavioural patterns of women in the work situation and in the community life. These together have strengthened the gender role stereotyping affecting the socio-economic status of women adversely. Hence, within the broad context of society, the resistance and articulation of individual woman like Parbati has no significant scope of expression.

The process of sanskritisation reinforces gender role stereotyping because it specifically recognises the life-style of the upper caste women as ideal womanhood. This process, however, recognises institutional forms of social interaction and binds women with the bondage of traditional values and norms. Resistance to these norms is considered unbecoming of a female.

Institutional political parties have been important agencies for political socialisation of the rural folk. They take the initiative to orient the rural people towards the political processes of parliamentary democracy in terms of the exercise of adult franchise in electoral politics. Besides, they socialise the rural folk to use institutionalised means to find out solutions to their problems. Though working-class women are significantly mobilised for collective actions, the process of their mobilisation is conditioned by these institutionalised norms. Since change is perceived as a gradual process the old norms and values are reinforced, in one form or another in the process of collective mobilisation. Undoing exploitative/discriminatory institutions is thus hampered. Working-class women may be mobilised for strikes against low wages and wage discrimination, but wage discrimination still persists in most villages. At the end of the strike the political leaders settle with the landowners for a marginal increase in the wages while ignoring gender-based wage discrimination. A Leftist party worker says:

> Under the present circumstances it is not possible to eradicate sexual wage discrimination. What we are trying is to make the rural women folk aware about their own issues.

The leadership of the mobilisation at the village level is mostly provided by male political workers. Though, in the recent years, with the formation of the women's wing of various political parties, the number of women activists has increased at the village level, the number of women leaders belonging to the agricultural working class are very few and far between. Hence, the ideas and expectations of these women remain overshadowed on many occasions. Maloti Kamanni, a 40-year old Scheduled Caste woman says.

> We are made to be hungry dogs. We run after dry bread. Sometimes, bread is thrown in front of us by the landowners, sometimes by the party leaders. We run after everybody with our begging bowls but lastly we find that no body has given us sufficient bread to meet our

> hunger. Rather, we have lost our begging bowls. . . . Who thinks about us? Even the party leaders do not realise the extent of our starvation, our problems. . . . We don't want our wage to be increased by 25 or 50 paise. We want Saman Saman Majuri (equal wage) and no wage variation by season. They don't consult us before coming to an understanding with the landowners. . .. When they need us to vote, to join meetings, processions and Gherao they come to us, we follow them, they don't care about our problems.

The age-old arrangement which has marginalised the economic status of working-class women in the rural society thus persists in the agrarian social structure in spite of repeated collective mobilisation against it. As women's marginalisation continues in the wage structure, similar marginalisation also continues in the aspects of women's access to property. We have already shown how women's marginal access to property has been institutionalised in so far as the distribution of surplus vested lands, implementation of Operation Barga and providing institutional loans are concerned. Against this backdrop the process of political socialisation has put certain limitations on the aspirations and collective resistance of women.

The Leftist party workers have initiated literacy programme for the adult rural women under the auspices of the Adult Education Programme. Adult Education Centres for women have been operating with substantial enrolment of agricultural working-class women in some agriculturally developed villages. Gender roles are conceived in the learning processes there. They are taught to be good mothers and housewives by maintaining minimum nutritional level for their children, keeping the house, utensils and the clothes clean, etc. The adult women students of these centres tend to be "lady-like" following the hair-style, manner of speech and dress of the female instructors. Gender roles typical to womanhood are significantly emphasised and reinforced in these education programmes.

Basis of Diversities in Women's Response to Contemporary Peasant Movement. Contemporary agrarian society of West Bengal faces diversified socio-economic conditions. The development strategy which aimed to smoothe the processes of agricultural modernisation and economic development, in reality has augmented regional disparities, sharpened inequality among the peasantry and affected the status of women in society adversely. Against this backdrop, the agrarian society has experienced diverse women's response in the processes of collective political mobilisation in the villages under reference. To provide an explanation to these varied forms and extent of women's response to collective mobilisation we are required to develop an understanding on the broad processes of the socio-economic transformations of the villages under enquiry.

The villages under category 'A' have achieved distinctly greater agricultural modernisation, economic development and rate of social change than village under category 'B' . The latter are characterised by wide-scale use of backward and traditional tools and technologies of cultivation, predominance of subsistence crop cultivation, prevalence of traditional moneylending system, presence of beck-and-call relationship, seasonal out-migration of the labour households and lack of elaborate market nexus. Agriculture has remained the main means of livelihod to most villagers. In the 'A' category villages the major trends are towards the wide-scale use of sophisticated and modern tools and technology of cultivation, predominantly cash crop and commodity cultivation, elaborate market network and prevalence of contractual social relationships, decline in the importance of beck-and-call relationships and traditional moneylending. Various avenues of economic activities alternative to agriculture have also opened up.

Against the given diversified backdrop it is not possible to identify a single mode of production in the agriculture of West Bengal. Various authors (Bhaduri 1973, Prasad 1973, Chandra 1974, Sau 1975 and others) have emphasised the prevalence of the semi-feudal legacy in agriculture especially in the eastern part of the country. They argue that elements of feudalism exist in agriculture, such as the reactionary role of usurious capital, predominant use of backward tools and technology, prevalence of sharecropping system, and extra-economic relations. Ashok Rudra (1971 and 1978) points out the capitalist form of agricultural development in some southern districts of West Bengal. He locates the facets of capitalist development in agriculture in terms of its large-scale commercialisation, use of scientific tools and technology, and emergence of contractual social relationships. Our study suggests, however, that the development in agriculture in West Bengal is not unidirectional. Variations do exist between the southern and northern regions of the state. The agrarian society of West Bengal is in a transitional phase and the modes of production have been many. Within this broad process of socio-economic formation women's response of collective mobilisation has also been diversely intertwined with the levels of economic development, agricultural modernisation and occupational diversifications of the state and society.

The economic foundation of society has widely affected the pattern of working-class women's response to the contemporary peasant movement. In the 'B' category villages due to persisting agricultural backwardness and non-availability of alternative avenues of employment, working-class women suffer extreme poverty, economic insecurity, unemployment and drudgery in work. They have, therefore, been united on the basis of common objective conditions:

(a) Agriculture is the only avenue of employment to most of them.
(b) They have common economic interests against the big landowners.
(c) They are underpaid.
(d) They are subject to gender-based wage discrimination.
(e) They either take seasonal out-migration or are tied up with beck-and-call relationship with the landowners.
(f) They suffer from extreme economic insecurity, poverty and unemployment.
(g) They are mostly from the landless or semi-landless households.
(h) They belong to the bottom of the caste hierarchy or to the tribal groups.

These rural women frequently accept the political path of agitation to get immediate economic gain. Indeed, the facets of their response are closely related to their shared identities with poverty and economic insecurity.

In the 'A' category villages, on the other hand, in the given processes of rapid agricultural modernisation, economic development, and occupational diversification, a significant section of agricultural working class women have accepted non-agricultural economic activities as an important source of their income. The working-class women have been socially disintegrated. The objective conditions of their life are not uniform. Thus,

(a) There have been diversities in their occupational patterns.
(b) Only one section of them work as agricultural wage earners and have an economic interest against the landowners.
(c) Only one section of them is primarily attached to wage earning for their mainstay, while others are employed in non-agricultural pursuits.
(d) An important section of them has been able to get gainful employment in the non-agricultural sector.

While political activists have tried to mobilise these women against the big landowners, the economic interests of all sections of them are not adequately represented in their manifesto of collective mobilisation. Their non-spontaneous and sporadic participation in collective mobilisation therefore depends on their diversified economic interests. Here only a small section of women whose economic positions are extremely insecure and whose interests are attached to agriculture respond regularly in the process of collective mobilisation.

Economic insecurity contributes significantly to the accumulation of the deprivation syndrome among rural women. But their discontent does not get adequate expression in the ideological framework of contemporary peasant movement. Their participation in it is, therefore, not necessarily stimulated by its ideological appeal but is more a matter of their urge to fulfil their familial needs. Those who find in contemporary peasant movement the hope of fulfilment of their familial economic security participate in it, not otherwise. That explains the significant correlationships between the economic position of working class women of the backward and developed villages.

There is no denial to the fact that the political parties have emerged to be the strong agents of social change in the rural areas; and that the political ideologies have provided broad perspective to the nature and direction of this change. However, in the process of institutionalisation and politicisation of the whole gamut of agrarian relationship the political ideological appeal of social change has not got uniform receptivity, among all sections of the working population, especially in the context of mass mobilisation. It is true that the ideological differences prevailing among the left political parties (that of the CPI, CPI(M), RSP etc.) are of very little significance to the working-class women. But the political rivalry, conflict and tension manifested in concrete form among the local political leaders caused enormous confusion in the mind of the working-class. This process is furthered by frequent defection of local political party leaders from one organisation and ideological fold to another and also by the inclusion of the formerly, noted 'class enemies' (Congress activists, rural rich, criminals) to the Leftist party fold. Hence confusion of the working-class women is generally culminated into the shift in their political loyalty from one political party to another. Thus in the whole process, on the one hand, the diversified economic interests have brought disintegration among the working-class rural women, on the other the ideology of the contemporary peasant movement and the political party activities have given very limited scope to them for the expression of their latent discontent against the accumulated deprived syndrome. The institutional norms and values of the society have smoothened these processes, adversely affecting the status of women in the society. Thus, while the social organisation of the rural life reels under the wheel of institutionalisation, the traditional patriarchal values and other normative arrangements of the society make their own space for the subjugation of women in the society.

It is, however, relevant to mention here that the extent of women's subjugation and the resultant manifestation of their discontent are not to be seen mechanically only in the contexts of economic conditions of existence, normative arrangements of the society and the ideology of mass mobilisation. The exogenous forces like education, urban contact, mass media, legislative measures etc. have composite bearings on the economic and organisational life of the working class. Again local issues are also interlinked to the macro social processes through regular state intervention, ideological penetration and mass mobilisation. Against this backdrop the form and extent of women's response to the peasant movement, whether historic or contemporary, can not be understood in terms of a one-to-one relationship. In this study we have developed a broad analytical perspective based on empirical reality. We have examined the form and direction of rural working-class women's response in terms of the ideological orientation of the movements under reference and the existing socio-economic realities of society which largely define the role and status of women in that society. The study suggests that women's response to peasant movements is patterned not simply by the contextual conditions, but by the interplay of the multiple endogenous and exogenous forces, and the micro and macro social processes as well.

SELECT BIBLIOGRAPHY

Agarwal, B.	1983	*Women's Studies in Asia and Pacific., An Overview of Current Status and Needed Priorities*, Kuala Lumpur: APDC.
————	1984	" Rural Women and High Yielding Variety Rice Technology" *E.P.W.**, XIX (13), pp. 39-52, pp. A-155-165.
————	1985	"Work Participation of Rural Women in Third World: Some Data and Conceptual Biases", *E.P.W.* XX (51-52) pp. A-155-165.
Alexander, K.C.	1975	*Agrarian Tension in Thanjavur*, Hyderabad: National Institute of Community Development.
Alavi, H.	1975	" India and Colonial Mode of Production", *E.P.W.*, X (33-35), pp. 1235-62.
Amin, S.	1984	"Of Peasant and Peasant Movement," *E.P.W.*, XIX (1) pp. 23-37.
Awasty, I.	1982	*Rural Women in India: A Socio-Economic Profile of Jammu Women*, New Delhi : B.R. Publishing Corporation.
Banaji, J.	1972	"For the Theory of Colonial Mode of Production", *E.P.W.*, VII (52), pp. 2498-2502.
Benedict, R.	1946	*Patterns of Culture*, New York: New American Library.
Banerjee, A.C.	1980	*The Agrarian System of Bengal*, Vol. 1, Calcutta: K.P. Bagchi.
Banerjee, A.K.	1972	*West Bengal District Gazetteers, Hooghly*, Calcutta : Govt. of West Bengal.

**Economic and Political Weekly* (Bombay)

Banerjee, N. 1979 "Politicization of Women in West Bengal", in Mazumder, V. (ed.), *Symbols of Power: Studies on the Political Status of Women in India,* New Delhi: Allied Publishers, pp. 164-72.

———— 1982 "Women and Poverty: Report on a Workshop", *E.P.W.*, XVIII (40), pp. 1693-98.

Bardhan, K. 1985 "Women's Work, Welfare and Status: Forces of Tradition and Change in India", *E.P.W.*, XX(50), pp. 2207-17.

Bardhan, P. 1978 "Some Employment and Unemployment Characteristics of Rural Women: An Analysis of NSS Data for West Bengal 1972-73", *E.P.W.*, Review of Agriculture, March, pp. A-21-26.

Bardhan, P. and A. Rudra 1980 "Types of Labour Attachment in Agriculture: Result of a Survey in West Bengal - 1979", *E.P.W.*, XV (35), pp. 1477-84.

———— 1985 "The Domain of Rural Labour Markets: Results of a Survey in West Bengal 1981-82", *E.P.W.*, XV (21-22), pp. A-153-54.

Basu, A. 1981 "Two Faces of Protest: Alternative Forms of Women's Mobilization in West Bengal and Maharashtra", in Minault, G. (ed.), *The Extended Family: Women and Political Particiaption in India and Pakistan*, New Delhi: Chanakya Publications.

Beteille, A. 1974 *Studies in Agrarian Social Structure*, New Delhi: Oxford University Press.

———— 1976 "The Position of Women in Indian Society", in Jain, D. (ed.), *Indian Women*, New Delhi: Ministry of Information and Broadcasting.

———— 1983 *The Idea of Natural Inequalities and other Essays*, New Delhi: Oxford University Press.

Bhaduri, A. 1973 "A Study of Agricultural Backwardness Under Conditions of Semi-feudalism", *Economic Journal*, 83 (329), pp. 120-37.

Blumer, H. 1951 "Social Movements", in Lee A.M. (ed.),

New Outline of Principles of Society, New York: Baines D. Noldi.

Bose, P.K. 1984 "Peasant Production and Capitalist Enterprise", *E.P.W.*, XIX (40), pp. 1747-54.

Boserup, E. 1970 *Women's Role in Economic Development*, London : George Allen & Unwin.

——— 1976 "Women in Labour Market", in Jain, D. (ed.), *Indian Women*, New Delhi: Publication Division, Ministry of Information and Broadcasting.

Bottomore, T.B. et al. (eds.) 1983 *A Dictionary of Marxian Thought*, Padstow, T.J. Press.

Boulding, E. 1976 *The Underside of History: A View of Women Through Time*, Colorado: Westview Press.

Braverman, J. 1974 *Labour and Monopoly Capitalism*, New York: Monthly Review Press.

Byres. T.J. 1981 "New Technology, Class Formation and Class Action in the Indian Country Side", *The Journal of Peasant Studies* , 8(4), pp. 405-54.

Centre for Studies in Social Sciences 1983 *Workshop on Women and Poverty*, Calcutta: CSSS.

Centre for Women's Development Studies (CWDS). 1983 *The Report of UGC Winter Institute for Orientation and Training of Teachers in Women Studies*, Bombay: RCWS.

Chakravarty, R. 1980 *Communists in Indian Women's Movement*, New Delhi: Peoples Publishing House.

Chandra, N. 1974 "Farm Efficiency Under Semi-feudalism: A Critique of Marginalist Theories and Some Marxist Formulation", *E.P.W.*, IX. (32-34), pp. 1309-13.

Chatterjee, P. 1982 Agrarian Structure in Pre-partition Bengal, in Sen, A.O., P. Chatterjee and P. Mukherjee, (eds.), *Perspective in Social Sciences*, Calcutta: Oxford University Press, pp. 113-222.

Chattopadhyay, B. 1981 "Notes Towards an Understanding of Bengal Famine of 1943", *Transactions*(1), pp. 112-53.

Chattopadhyay, M.	1982	"Role of Female Làbour in Indian Agriculture", *Social Scientist*, 10(7), pp. 43-54.
Chattopadhyay, P.	1972	"On the Question of Mode of Production in Indian Agriculture: A Preliminary Note", *E.P.W.*, Review of Agriculture, March, pp. 39-46.
Chattopadhyay, S.	1979	"Operation Barga: A Comment", *E.P.W.*, XIV, pp. 2022 -24
Chaudhuri, B.	1977	*Banglar Bhumi Babasthar Ruparekha* (in Bengali) (An Outline of Bengals Land System) Calcutta: National Book Agency.
Chadhuri, B.B.	1979	" Agrarian Movements in Bengal and Bihar: 1919-1939", in Desai, A.R. (e.d.), *Peasant Struggles in India*, Bombay: Oxford University Press, pp: 336-74.
Chaudhuri, R.B.	1981	*The British Agrarian Policy in Eastern India (Bengal and Bihar)*, Patna: Janki Prakashan.
Committee on the Status of Women in India (CSWI)	1974	*Towards Equality*, New Delhi, Ministry of Education and Social Welfare, Govt. of India.
CPI (M.L.) Santosh Rana Group	1985	*Nari Mukti Andolaner Ruparekha* (in Bengali) (An Outline of Women's Liberation in India) (unpublished), Gopiballavpur, West Bengal.
Custers, P.	1986	"Women's Role in Tebhaga Movement", *E.P.W.*, XXI (43), pp. WS 97-104.
Dahlstrom, E. & Liljestorm, R.,	1983	"The Patriarchal Heritage and the Working Class Women", *Acta Sociologica*, 26 (1), pp. 3-20.
Dasgupta, B.	1974	*The Naxalite Movement*, New Delhi: Allied Publishers.
————	1984	"Sharecropping in West Bengal: From Independence to Operation Barga", *E.P.W.*, XIX (26), pp. A-85-96.
Davin, D.	1976	*Women ,Work and the Party in Revolutionary China*, London: Oxford University Press.
Delamant, S.	1980	*The Sociology of Women: An Introduction*,

London: George Allen & Unwin.

Desai, A.R. 1979 *Peasant Struggles in India*, Bombay: Oxford University Press.

———— 1985 "Women's Movement in India: An Assessment", *E.P.W.* (23), pp. 992-94.

de Souza, A.(ed.) 1980 *Women in Contemporary India and South Asia*, New Delhi: Manohar.

Dhanagare, D.N. 1976 Peasant Protest and Politics—The Tebhaga Movement in Bengal (India) 1946-47), *Journal of Peasant Studies*, 3 (3), pp. 613-14.

Donofrio-Flores, P. Pamela & S.M. Pfafflin (eds.) 1983 *Scientific Technological Change and Role of Women in Development*, Colorado: Westview Press.

Dorner, P. 1972 *Land Reform and Economic Development*, England: Penguin Books.

D'Souza V. 1980 "Family Status and Female Work Participation", in de Souza, A. (ed.), *Women in Contemporay India and South Asia*, New Delhi: Manohar.

Dube , L. 1988 "Socialisation of Hindu Girls in Patrilineal India", in Chanana, K. (ed.), *Socialisation, Education and Women*, New Delhi: Orient Longman.

Dunne, F. 1980 "Occupational Sex Stereo-typing among Rural Young Women and Men", *Rural Sociology* , 45 (3), pp. 396-415.

Durkheim, E. 1933 *Division of Labour in the Society*, New York: The Free Press.

Encyclopaedia of Britannica Inc. (EBI) 1977 *The New Encyclopedia of Britannica*, Chicago: William Benton.

Engles, F. 1976 *The Origin of the Family, Private Property and the State*, Karl Marx & Frederic Engels Selected Works. Vol. 3. Moscow : Progress Publishers.

Ericksen, J.&G. Klein 1981 Women's Roles in Family Production among the Old Order Amish", *Rural Sociology* , 46(2), pp. 282-96.

Famine Commission 1945 *Report of the Famine Enquiry Commission*, Calcutta: Government of Bengal.

Forbes, G.H. 1979 "The Women's Movement in India: Traditional Symbols and New Roles", in M.S.A. Rao (ed.), *Social Movements in India*, New Delhi: Manohar.

Freudenbury 1981 "Women and Men in an Energy Boomtown: Adjustment, Alienation and Adoptation", *Rural Sociology* , (46), pp. 220-44.

Gadgil, D.R. 1924 *The Industrial Evolution in India in Recent Times*, Bombay: Oxford University Press.

——— 1965 *Women in the Working Force in India*, Calcutta: Asia Publishing House.

Gandhi, M.K. 1936 *Message to the All India Women's Conference: The Collected Works of Mahatma Gandhi*, Ahmedabad: Navjivan Trust, Vol. L XIV, p.165.

Gangrade, K.D. 1983 Employment of Women and Children: Battles to Fight", in Gangrade, K.D. & J.A. Gathia (eds.) , *Women and Child Workers in Unorganised Sector*, New Delhi: Concept Publishing House.

Gangrade, K.D. & J.A. Gathia (eds.) 1983 *Women and Child Workers in Unorganised Sector*, New Delhi: Concept Publishing Company.

Garnsey, E. 1978 "Women's Work and Theories of Class Stratification", *Sociology*, (12), pp. 223-43.

Ghosh, R. 1979 "Land Reform and the Draft Five Year Plan: 1978-1982, *E.P.W.*, XIV. (45), pp. 1950-55.

Ghosh & Dutta 1977 *Development of Capitalist Relations in Agriculture: A Case Study in W.B. 1793-1971*, New Delhi: Peoples Publishing House.

Goode, W.J. 1968 *Religion among the Primitives*, New York: The Free Press.

Govt. of India 1931 *Census of India* (Census of Bengal Province), Calcutta: Govt. of India Press.

——— 1956 *Report of the Committee of the Panel on Land Reform*, New Delhi: Govt. of India Press.

——— 1961 *Census of India*, New Delhi: Ministry of

Broadcasting & Publication..

———— 1971 *Census of India*, New Delhi: Ministry of Broadcasting & Publication.

———— 1975 *Rural Labour Enquiry*, New Delhi: Ministry of Labour, Govt. of India.

———— 1975 *International Women's Year: World Conference on International Women's Year. Maxico City*, New Delhi: Ministry of Education & Social Welfare, Govt. of India.

———— 1976 *International Women's Year*, New Delhi: Ministry of Education & Social Welfare, Govt. of India.

———— 1979 *Report of the National Conference on Women & Development*, New Delhi: Women's Welfare & Development Bureau.

———— 1981 *Census of India*, New Delhi: Ministry of Broadcasting and Publication, Govt. of India.

———— 1985 *India 1985*, New Delhi: Ministry of Information and Broadcasting, Govt. of India.

———— 1986 *Seventh Five Year Plan*, New Delhi : Govt. of India Press.

Govt. of W.B. 1978 *Workshop on Land Reform*, Calcutta: Board of Revenue, Govt., of West Bengal.

———— 1980 *Pachimbanga*, Calcutta.

———— 1980 *Report on Land Reform*, Calcutta: *Govt of West Bengal.*

———— 1980 *West Bengal Land Reforms Act 1955*, Calcutta : Govt. of West Bengal.

———— 1980 *West Bengal Estate Acquisition Act 1953. (as amended up-to-date)*, Calcutta: Govt. of West Bengal.

———— 1984 *Pachimbange Bam Front Sarkar*, (in Bengali) (Left Front Govt. in West Bengal), Calcutta: Deptt. of Culture and Information, Govt. of West Bengal.

———— 1985 *Report on Land Reform*, Calcutta: Govt of West Bengal.

Guesfield, J.R. (ed) 1971 *Protest, Reform and Revolt: New York: A*

		Reader in Social Movements, New York: John Wiley and Sons.
————	1972	"The Study of Social Movements", *International Encyclopedia of Social Sciences*, New York: Macmillan Company and Free Press.
Gujral, S.	1976	"India's Rural Women", in Vashishta (ed.), *Encyclopeadia of Women in India*. New Delhi: Praveen Encyclopaedia Publication.
Gulati, L.	1975	"Sex Discrimination in Work and Wages", *Social Scientist*, 4(4-5), pp. 155-60.
————	1978	Profile of a Female Agricultural Labourer", *E.P.W.*, Review of Agriculture, March, pp. 30-35.
————	1984	"Technological Change, Women's Work Participation and Demographic Behaviour: A Case Study of Three Fishing Villages", *E.P.W.* , XIX (49), pp. 2089-94.
Gupta, A.	1979	"Mobilizing Women for Change", *Social Scientist*, 8(88).
Haberle, R.	1951	*Social Movements*, New York: Appleton Century-Crofts.
————	1972	"Types and Functions of Social Movements", *International Encyclopedia of Social Sciences*, New York : Macmillan Company Free Press.
Hamilton, W.	1928	*The East India Gazetteer*, New Delhi: B.R. Publishing Corporation.
Harris, J.	1977	"Capitalism and Peasant Farming", *E.P.W.* XVIII (49), pp. 1961-68.
Haque, A.	1939	*Man Behind the Plough*, Calcutta.
Haymai, H.	1981	"Agrarian Problems of India: An East and South East Asian Perspective", *E.P.W.* , XVI (16), pp 707-12.
His Majesty's Authority (rpt)	1959	*Imperial Gazetteer of India*, New Delhi: Today and Tomorrow's Printers and Publishers, Vol. VII.
Honig, E.,	1985	"Socialist Revolution and Women's Liberation in China", *The Journal of Asian Studies*, XLIV (2), pp. 229-336.

Hunter, W.W, (rpt.) 1973 *A Statistical Account of Bengal*, New Delhi: D.K. Publishing House, Vol. III.

Indian Council of Social Science Research (ICSSR) 1977 (a) *Programme of Women Studies*, New Delhi: ICSSR

——— 1977 (b) *Critical Issues on the Status of Women*, New Delhi: ICSSR.

Islam, M.M., 1978 *Bengal Agriculture: 1920-1946*, New Delhi: S. Chand & Co.

Jain, D., 1980 *Women's Quest for Power*, Ghaziabad: Vikas Publishing House.

Jose, A.V., 1984 "Farm Mechanization in Asian Countries: Some Perspectivs", *E.P.W.*, XIX (26) pp. A-97-103

Joshi, P.C., 1969 "Land Reform in India", in Desai A.R. (ed.), *Rural Sociology in India*, Bombay: Popular Prakasan, pp. 444-74.

——— 1982 "Technology and Agricultural Transformation", *Link*, 25, (1), pp. 67-71.

Kannabiran V, and K. Lalitha 1989 "That Magic Time: Women in the Telengana Peoples Struggle", in Sangri, K. & S.D. Vaid (eds.), *Recasting Women: Essays in Colonial History*, New Delhi: Kali for Women.

Khan, A.M. & N. Ayesha 1982 *Status of Rural Women in India*, New Delhi: Uppal Publishing House.

Karlekar, M. 1983 "Women's Studies in Eighties: State of the Discipline in the U.S.A. and India", *Samya Shakti*, 1(1), pp. 11-15.

Kelkar, G. & S. Anandalakshmy 1980 *Role of Women in Post Harvesting Food Conservation Care: Study of a Village in Haryana*, Tokyo: United Nation's University.

Kernea, M. 1978 "Macro Social Change, Feminization of Agriculture and Peasant Women's Threefold Role", *Sociologia Ruralis*, 18 (182), pp. 107-24.

Kotovsky, G. 1964 *Agrarian Reforms in India*, New Delhi: Peoples Publishing House.

Lamphere, L.	1975	"Women and Domestic Power: Political and Economic Strategies of Domestic Groups", in Raphel, D (ed.), *Being Female Reproduction, Power and Change*, Paris: Mouton, pp. 117-30.
Land Revenue Commission (LRC)	1940	*Report of the Land Revenue Commission*, 1940, Calcutta: Govt. of Bengal, Bengal Govt. Press.
Law, P.	1985	Rural Development: Its Impact on Women" *Social Action* , 35(1), pp. 81-90.
Left Front	1982	*Bam Fronter Nirbachani Estahar* (in Bengali) (Election Manifesto of the Left Front), Calcutta: U.L.F.
Lenin, V.I.	1970	*Collected Works*, Vol. 9, Moscow: Progress Publishers.
Levi Stauss, C.	1949	*The Elementary Structure of Kinship*, London: Social Science Paperback.
Linares, O.F.	1985	"Cash-Crops and Gender Constructs: The Jola of Senegal", *Ethnology* , XVIV (2) , pp. 83-84.
Lenski, G.E.	1966	*Power and Privilege*, New York: McGraw Hill.
Linton, R.	1971	"On Status and Role", in Truzz M. (ed.), *Sociology: The Classic Movement*, New York: Random House.
Lowie, R.H.	1920	*Primitive Society*, New York: Liveright.
Malinowski, B.	1927	*Sex and Repression in Savage Society*, London: Routledge & Kegan Paul.
Maloba, W.	1983	"The Women in Africa", *Dialectical Anthropology* , 7 (4), pp. 315-27.
Man, E.G.	1983	*Sonthalia & The Sonthals*, New Delhi: Mittal Publications.
Manohar, K.M.	1982	"Socio-economic Status of Indian Women", in Manohar, K.M. (ed.), *Socio-Economic Status of Indian Women*, New Delhi: Seema Publications.
Maret, E. & L. Chenoweth	1976	*The Labour Force Patterns of Mature Rural Women, Rural Sociology,* 44 (4), pp. 736-53.

Marx, K. 1976 *Selected Works*, Vol. III, Moscow: Progress Publishers.

Mazumdar, V. 1978 "Towards Equality Status: of Women in India", in Phadnis U. & I. Malni (eds.), *Women of the World*, New Delhi : Vikas Publishing House, pp: 17-29.

———— (ed.) 1979 *Symbols of Power : Studies in the Political Status of Women in India*, New Delhi: Allied Publishers.

———— (ed.) 1983(a) *Women and Rural Transformation*, New Delhi: Concept Publishing House.

———— 1983(b) "The Role of Research in Women's Development: A Case Study of ICSSR Programme of Women's Studies", *Samya Shakti*, 1 (1), pp. 24-42.

Mazumdar V., K. Sharma, & S. Acharya 1979 *Country Review and Analysis on the Role and Participation of Women in Agriculture and Rural Development in India*, New Delhi: ICSSR.

Mead, M. 1931 *Growing up in New Guinea: A Study of Adolescence and Sex in Primitive Societies*, Harmondsworth, U.K.: Penguin Books.

Mencher, J.P. 1974 "Problems of Analysing Rural Class-Structure", *E.P.W.* , IX (35), pp. 1495-1503.

Mitchel, G.D. 1968 *A Dictionary of Sociology*, London: Routledge and Kegan Paul.

Mukhopadhyay, A. 1979 *Operation Barga, E.P.W.* ,(37), pp. 1566-67.

Mukherjee, P.N. 1978 "Naxalbari Movement and Peasant Revolt in North Bengal", in Rao, M.S.A. (ed.), *Social Movement in India*, New Delhi: Manohar.

———— 1979 *From Extremism to Electoral Politics: Naxalite Participation in Elections*, New Delhi: Manohar.

Mukherjee, P.N. & M. Chattopadhyay 1981 "Agrarian Structure, Proletarianization and Social Mobilization", *Sociological Bulletin*, 30 (2), pp. 137-62.

Mukherjee, R. 1957 *Dynamics of a Rural Society*, Berlin: Academic Verlag.

Mukherjee, R.K., 1933 *Land Problems of India*, Calcutta: Calcutta University Press.

Mukhopadhyay, S., 1981 "Women Workers in India: A Case of Market Segmentation", in ILO (ed.), *Women in the Indian Labour Force*, Geneva: ILO.

Murdock, G.P. 1949 *Outline of World Culture*, New York: The Free Press.

Myrdal, A. 1941 *Nation and Family: The Swedish Experiment in Democratic Family and Population Policy*, Cambridge: The MIT Press.

Myrdal, A. & V. Klein 1968 *Women's Two Roles: Home and Work*, London: Routledge & Kegan Paul.

Myrdal, G. 1968 *Asian Drama: An Enquiry into the Poverty of the Nation*, London: Penguin Press, Vol. 2.

Nadel, S.F. 1969 *The Theory of Social Structure*, London: Cohen & West.

Nagbrahman, D. & S. Sambrani, 1983 "Women's Drudgery in Firewood Colection", *E.P.W.*, XIIII (182), pp. 33-38.

National Sample Survey Organisation (NSSO) 1952 1962 1972 *National Sample Survey*, New Delhi: NSSO.

Omvedt, G. 1977 "Women and Rural Revolt in India", *Journal of Peasant Studies*, 5, pp. 370-403.

Oommen, T.K. 1984 *Social Transformation in Rural India*, New Delhi: Vikas Publishing House.

Oppong, C. 1980 *A Synopsis of Seven Roles and Statuses of Women: An Outline of a Conceptual and Methodological Approach*, Geneva: ILO.

Palmer, I. 1984 *Case Studies of the Impact of Large Scale Development Project on Women*, New York: Population Council.

Parthasarathy, G. & G.D. Rao 1981 "Women in the Labour Force in India", in ILO (Ed.), *Women in Indian Labour Force*, Geneva: ILO.

Patnaik, U. 1971 "Capitalist Development in Indian Agriculture," *E.P.W.*, VI (39), pp. 123-30.

——— 1972 "On Mode of Production in Indian Agriculture: A Reply", *E.P.W.*, VII (40), pp. 145-51.

Paxtion, J. (ed.)	1980	*The Statesman Year Book*, 1980-81.
National Commission on Agriculture (NCA)	1976	*Report of the National Commission on Agriculture*, New Delhi: Ministry of Agriculture and Irrigation, Govt. of India.
Prasad, P.	1973	"Production Relations: Achilles Heal of Indian Planning" , *E.P.W.*, VIII (19), pp. 869-72.
————	1974	"Reactionary Role of Usurers Capital in Rural India", *E.P.W.*, IX (32-34), pp. 1305-1309.
Redcliffe-Brown A.R.	1922	*The Andaman Islanders*, New York: The Free Press.
————	1952	*Structure and Functions in Primitive Society*, London: Cohen & West.
Raghuramaiah, L.	1976	"Emergence of Modern Indian Womenhood", in Vashishta, B.K. (ed.), *Encyclopaedia of Women in India*, New Delhi: Praveen Encyclopaedia Publication, pp. 70-86.
Raphael, D.	1975	"Women and Power: Introductory Notes", in Raphael, D. (ed.), *Being Female Reproduction Power and Change*, Paris: Mouton, pp. 111-15.
Rao, M.S.A.	1979	*Social Movements and Social Transformation*, Madras: Macmillan.
Rao, V.S.	1986	"Rural Labour: A Case Study of Karnataka Village", *E.P.W.* , XIX (18), pp. 766-76.
Rasul, M.A.	1974	*A History of All India Kisan Sabha*, Calcutta: National Book Agency.
Ray, R.	1988	*The Naxalites and Their Ideology*, New Delhi: Oxford University Press.
Rothschild, J.	1981	"Technology, Women's Work and Social Control of Women", in Randel M. (ed.), *Women Power and Political Systems*, London: Croom Helm, pp. 160-83.
Roy, M.	1975(a)	"Concept of Feminity and Liberation in the Context of Changing Sex Roles: Women in Modern India and America", in Raphael, D. (ed.), *Being Female Reproduction, Power and Change*, Paris: Mouton, pp. 218-30.

———— 1975(b) *Bengali Women,* London: University of Chicago Press.

Roychaudhuri, P. 1980 "Land Reforms: Promise and Fulfilment", *E.P.W.*, XV (52), pp. 2171-74.

Rudra, A. 1971 "Capitalist Development in Agriculture-Reply", *E.P.W.*, VI(45), pp. 2251-92.

———— 1974 "Semi-Feudalism, Usury Capital Etcetera", *E.P.W.* , IX (48), pp. 1996-97.

———— 1978 "Class Relations in Indian Agriculture", *E.P.W.* , XIII (22, 23, 24), pp. 916-23, 963-68, 998-1003.

Safilios-Rothschild C. 1985 "The Persistence of Women's Invisibility in Agriculture: Theoretical and Policy Lessons from Lesotho and Sierra Leone", *Economic Development and Cultural Change*, 33(2), pp. 299-317.

Salamen, S. & A.M., Kein 1979 "Land Ownership and Woman's Power", *Marriage and Family*, 41(7), pp. 109-19,

Saradamoni, K. 1983 "Changing Land Relations and Women: A Case Study of Palghat District, Kerala", in Mazumdar, V. (ed.), *Women and Rural Transformation*, New Delhi: Concept Publishers, pp. 9-15.

Sarkar. T. 1984 "Politics and Women in Bengal: The Condition and Meaning of Participation", *The Indian Economic & Social Review* , XXI (1), pp. 91-102.

Savur, M. 1975 "Women's Liberation and Productive Activity", *Social Scientists*, IV (4-5), pp. 9-27.

Sau, R. 1975 "Political Economy of Indian Agriculture: What is it all about?, *E.P.W.* , X (20) , pp. 911-14.

Seal, K.C. 1981 "Women in the Labour Force in India: A Macro Level Statistical Profile", *Women in Indian Labour Force*, Geneva: ILO.

Self-Employed Women's Association 1981 *Report of National Workshop on Organising Self-Employed Women in India*, Ahmedabad: SEWA.

Sen, G.	1985	"Development, Crisis and Alternative Visions", *Third World Women's Perspectives: Development Alternatives with Women for a New Era*, New Delhi.
Sen, S.	1979a	*Agrarian Relations in India: 1793-1947*, New Delhi: Peoples Publishing House.
————	1979b	"The Kisan Sabha", in Desai, A.R. (ed.), *Peasant Struggles, in India*, Bombay: Oxford University Press, pp. 428-41.
————	1979c	"The Bargadars Bill", in Desai, A.R. (ed.), *Peasant Struggles, in India*, Bombay: Oxford University Press, pp. 453-60.
————	1979d	"Tebhaga Chi", in Desai, A.R. (ed.), *Peasant Struggles, in India*, Bombay: Oxford University Press, pp. 42-52.
————	1982	*Peasant Movements in India: Mid Nineteenth to Twentieth Centuries*, Calcutta: K.P. Bagchi.
————	1985	"The Working Women in West Bengal: A Study in Popular Movements and Women's Organisation", in ILO (ed.), *Rural Development and Women: Lesson from Field.* Geneva: ILO, pp. 249-66.
Sen G. and C. Sen	1985	"Women's Domestic Work and Economic Activity: Results from National Sample Survey",. *E.P.W.*, XX(17), pp. Ws-49-56.
Sengupta, B.,	1979	*CPI (M)—Promises, Prospects and Problems,* New Delhi: Young Asia Publications.
Sengupta, J.C.,	1965	*West Bengal District Gazetteers,West Dinajpur*, Calcutta : Govt. of West Bengal.
Sengupta, S.	1970	*A Study of Women of Bengal,* Calcutta: Indian Publication.
Sethi, R.M.	1982	*Female Labour in Agriculture : A Case Study of Punjab,* Chandigarh: Amrit Printing Press.
Shah, K.	1984	Caste, Class and Gender in Women's Struggle, Paper Presented in All India Sociological Conference, Surat.
Sharma, R.K.,	1981.	*Nationalism, Social Reform and Indian*

		Women, New Delhi: Janaki Prakashan.
Singh, K.S. & P.P. Mahato	1983	"The Mahato Kurmi Mahasabha Movement in Chotanagpur", in K.S. Singh (ed.), *Tribal Movements in India*, Vol. 2, New Delhi: Manohar, pp. 109-18.
Srinivas, M.N.	1978	*The Changing Position of Indian Women* , New Delhi: Oxford University Press.
Srivastava, S.C.	1971	*Indian Census in Perspective: Centenary Monograph, No.1*, New Delhi: Ministry of Home Affairs.
State Committee CPI (M)	1982	*Ai Abicharer Biruddhey Rukhey Dharan* (in Bengali), Protest Against this Injustice), Calcutta: W.B. State Committee, CPI (M).
————	1982	*Gourabujjal Panchti Bachar* (in Bengali), (The Glorious Five Years), Calcutta : W.B. State Committee, CPI(M).
————	1985	*West Bengal: Reports of CPI (M) and its Various Frontal Activities*, Calcutta: Ganashakti Printers.
Thorner, A.	1982	"Semi-feudalism or Capitalism: Contemporary Debate on the Class and Mode of Production in India", *E.P.W.*, XVIII (49, 50-51), pp. 1961-68, 1993-99, 2061-66.
Thorner, D.	1956	*Agrarian Prospects in India*, Bombay: Allied Publishers.
————	1969	"Capitalist Farm in India", *E.P.W.* , IV (52), pp. 2189-94.
————	1980	*The Shaping of Modern India*, New Delhi : Allied Publishers.
Thorner, D. & Alice	1962	*Land and Labour in India*, Bombay: Asia Publishing House.
————	1965	*The Working Force in India: 1881-1951, Part 1*, Bombay: Indian Statistical Institute.
Toch, H.	1965	*The Social Psychology of Social Movements*, Indianapolis: Bobbs-Merril.
UNESCO	1982	*Women's Studies in Social Sciences,* New Delhi: ICSSR.
United Nations	1975	*World Conference of the International*

		Women's Year, Conference Background Papers, Maxico City.
Visaria, P.	1976	"Employment: A Trend Report", in ICSSR (ed.), *A Survey of Research in Economics,* Vol. 2, New Delhi: Allied Publishers, pp. 125-209.
Warriner, D.	1969	*Land Reform in Principle and Practice,* Oxford: Clarendon Press.
W.B. C.A.D.C.	1980	*CADP Today,* Calcutta: West Bengal Comprehensive Area Development Corporation.
Weber, M.	1958	*The Protestant Ethics and the Spirit of Capitalism,* (Translated by T. Parson), New York: Charles Seribner's Sons.
Wilson, J.	1973	*Introduction to Social Movements,* New York: Basic Books.
Woodsmall. R.F.	1960	*Women and the New East,* Washington: The Middle East Institute.
Yoon, S.Y.	1983	"Women Studies: Is it Relevant?", *Samya Shakti,* 1(1), 1-10.

INDEX